M

∞

The Hidden Power
of Kindness

The Hidden Power of Kindness

A Practical Handbook for Souls
Who Dare to Transform the World,
One Deed at a Time

by the Reverend
Lawrence G. Lovasik

SOPHIA INSTITUTE PRESS®
Manchester, New Hampshire

Sophia Institute Press®
Box 5284, Manchester, NH 03108
1-800-888-9344
www.sophiainstitute.com

Imprimi potest: Very Rev. Raymond J. Weisenberger, S.V.D.
Provincial, Girard, Pennsylvania
Nihil obstat: Right Rev. Msgr. Wilfrid J. Nash, Litt.D.
Censor Librorum
Imprimatur: John Mark Gannon, D.D., D.C.L., LL.D.
Archbishop of Erie, Pennsylvania
May 27, 1961

Library of Congress Cataloging-in-Publication Data

Lovasik, Lawrence G. (Lawrence George), 1913-
    The hidden power of kindness : a practical handbook for souls who
dare to transform the world, one deed at a time / Lawrence G. Lovasik.
        p.   cm.
    Abridged ed. of: Kindness.
    ISBN 1-928832-00-8 (pbk. : alk. paper)
    1. Kindness — Religious Aspects — Catholic Church. I. Lovasik,
Lawrence G. (Lawrence George), 1913- Kindness. II. Title.
BV4647.K5 L68   1999
241'.4 — dc21   99-043436 CIP

99 00 01 02 03 10 9 8 7 6 5 4 3 2 1

∽

Contents

Part Three

Show your love in kind deeds

Appendix

Biographical Note

∞

Foreword

The world needs kindness. By being kind, we have the power of making the world a happier place in which to live, or at least we greatly diminish the amount of unhappiness in it so as to make it a quite different world.

The world is unkind only for the lack of kindness in the individuals who live in it. It is, therefore, worth your while to take the trouble to understand the real meaning of this virtue. You can practice more easily what you already know clearly.

There is no more genuine kindness than that which has its inspiration through the grace of God and in the perfect fulfillment of God's greatest law: "the royal law of charity." These chapters on kindness sincerely attempt to explain that law.

These pages are dedicated to the Sacred Heart of Jesus, Model and Source of true kindness and charity, and to the Immaculate Heart of Mary, the Mother of Mercy, who mirrors her Son so well.

Father Lawrence G. Lovasik
March 25, 1961
Divine Word Seminary
Girard, Pennsylvania

∞

*The Hidden Power
of Kindness*

Part One

∞

Develop a kind attitude

Chapter One

∽

Practice the elements
of kindness

The standard for the love of God is giving all. It reaches into the very depths of the powers of your soul. "Love the Lord your God with all your heart, and with all your soul, and with all your strength, and with all your mind."[1]

The standard for the love of neighbor is love of self. "Love your neighbor as yourself."[2]

You may have problems with the two short words *as yourself*, words too often overlooked. You should love others in the same measure as you love yourself — as if your neighbor were your very self. Such love is naturally kind.

When you are kind, you put others in the place of yourself. Self-love becomes unselfishness.

Kindness in God is the act of creation and the constant preservation of the world in existence. From divine kindness flow, as from a fountain, the powers and the blessings of all created kindness.

[1] Luke 10:27.
[2] Ibid.

Kindness also means coming to the rescue of others when they need help, if it is in our power to supply it. This, too, is the work of the attributes of God toward His creatures. His omnipotence is forever making up our deficiency of power. His justice is continually correcting our erroneous judgments. His mercy is always consoling our fellow creatures under our unkindnesses. His perfections are unceasingly coming to the rescue of our imperfections. This is Divine Providence.[3]

Kindness is our imitation of Divine Providence. Kindness, to be perfect and lasting, must be a conscious imitation of God. If you are earnestly conforming yourself to the image of Jesus Christ, sharpness, bitterness, and sarcasm disappear. The very attempt to be like Jesus is already a source of sweetness within you, flowing with an easy grace over all who come within your reach.

Not only is kindness due to everyone, but a *special* kindness is due to everyone. Kindness is not kindness unless it is special. Its charm consists in its fitness, its timeliness, and its individual application.

Kindness adds sweetness to everything. It makes life's capabilities blossom and fills them with fragrance. Kindness is like divine grace. It bestows on men something that neither self nor nature can give them. What it gives them is something of which they are in need, or something which only another person can give, such as consolation. Besides, the manner in which this is given is a true gift itself, better far than the thing given.

The secret impulse out of which kindness acts is an instinct that is the noblest part of yourself. It is the most undoubted remnant of the image of God, given to us at the beginning. Kindness

---

[3] Cf. Frederick William Faber, *Spiritual Conferences* (Baltimore: John Murphy Company, 1859), 19.

springs from the soul of man; it is the nobility of man — a divine rather than a human being.

∞

Kindness anticipates others' needs and wishes

Obligingness urges you to carry out a wish or satisfy need before a request is made. You will not wait for your neighbor to express a wish; you detect his need and kindly gratify his unspoken request.

When you comply with the spoken request of your neighbor, you may do so either because you do not wish to appear unkind, or because you feel unable to resist the persuasion of another, or because in this way you hope to rid yourself sooner of a troublesome person. But when you are truly obliging, love prompts gracious thoughts, tells you of your neighbor's wish, and urges you to comply with it. Here love alone pleads and complies with the wish. Hence, obligingness is an act of charity even more beautiful than a simple readiness to serve another.

Obligingness prevents you from becoming careless in charity, because it arouses charity to action. It is a constant striving to do good on your own initiative. Even though you comply more or less unwillingly with a request, the danger remains of your falling back into a spiritual carelessness.

Obligingness is an attractive form of charity. It has something divine about it. Most of God's gifts come to us without our asking for them. Long before weak man existed, God planned to call him to share in His everlasting bliss. Long before we could lift our hearts to pray, He created, redeemed, and sanctified us. St. John says, "In this the love of God was made manifest in us, that God sent His only Son into the world, so that we might live through Him. In this is love: not that we have loved God, but that he loved us and sent His Son to be the expiation for our sins. Beloved, if

God so loved us, we also ought to love one another."[4] Obliging-ness is a richer joy-giver than mere willingness to render service. A gift which is the result of a formal request nearly always loses something of its full value and, as a consequence, something of its power to give pleasure; whereas, anything done out of obliging love keeps undiminished its ability to make people happy. When a pure motive of charity inspires a gift, it never fails to produce much joy and bestow on the giver a rich blessing. The purer your love, the richer its natural and supernatural blessings. The more you give, the more you receive.

If you are a person of gentle feelings, you will attract others by a certain delicacy and attention to their small needs, by discovering their least desires and constantly forgoing your own, and by ren-dering little services even before they are requested. Do not wait for your neighbor to express a wish, but gratify his unspoken wish. Keep your eyes open to discover other people's needs; take the trouble to remove an obstacle in the path of another; let your hands be busy providing pleasant surprises for your neighbor; be eager to undertake things for others or run errands for them with-out waiting to be asked.

This is what it means to be obliging. This is genuine kindness that imitates the obliging love of God.

∞

Kindness counteracts the unhappiness of sin

God wants all men to be happy. He created us to show forth His goodness and to share in His happiness in Heaven someday. God gave you the power to be happy, and kindness is a great part of that very power.

[4] 1 John 4:9-11.

Kindness makes life more endurable. The burden of life presses heavily on most people. Many find life almost unbearable. Yet, to a virtuous man, sin alone is sufficient to make life unbearable.

We make ourselves more unhappy than other people make us. A great portion of this self-inflicted unhappiness arises from our sense of justice being so continually wounded by the events of life. Kindness steps forward to remedy this evil also, because kindness is the amiability of justice. Each kind action that you do works to restore the balance between right and wrong.

∞

Kindness has a powerful influence on others

Kindness is constantly winning stray souls back to God by opening hearts that seemed obstinately closed. "Kindness has converted more sinners than either zeal, eloquence, or learning; and these three last have never converted anyone, unless they were kind also."[5]

We often begin our own repentance by acts of kindness, or through them. Probably the majority of repentances have begun in the reception of acts of kindness, which touched men by the sense of their being so undeserved.

By kindness, you encourage others in their efforts after good. All of us need encouragement, and most of us must have praise. Kindness encompasses all the virtues of praise without its vices. When you are praised, you are praised at some expense, and at your own expense, for praise may encourage pride. But kindness puts you to no expense, and, at the same time, enriches those who are kind to you. Kindness is the most graceful attitude you can assume toward another, whereas praise implies some degree of

[5] Faber, *Spiritual Conferences*, 23.

9

condescension. Kindness is the only sort of praise that is always and everywhere true.

There are few things that resist grace so much as discouragement. Many plans for God's glory have failed because there was no bright look or kind eye or kind word to support them. You may not have come forward with the help your brother needs, because you were busy with your own work and never looked at his, or because you were jealous and looked coldly and spoke critically.[6]

A kind deed, a kind word, or the mere tone of voice is enough to convey sympathy to the poor suffering heart, and in one instant all is right again. The downcast soul is encouraged to do bravely the very thing which, in a mood of discouragement, it had almost resolved to leave undone. That encouragement may be the first link of a new chain, which, when finished, will result in final perseverance.

∞

A little kindness goes a long way

The amount of kindness bears no proportion to the *effect* of kindness. People generally do not look at what you have had to give up in order to do for them what you have done. They see only the kindness. It is not what you do, but how you do it that matters.

The least kind action is greater than the greatest wrong. The smallest kindness can lift a heavy weight. It reaches far and travels swiftly. And a kind action lasts a long time. The doing of it is only the beginning. Years of estrangement can hardly take the sweetness out of a kind deed.

The more you try to repay kind deeds, the further off you seem from having repaid them. The obligations of gratitude seem to

[6] Cf. Faber, *Spiritual Conferences*, 29.

lengthen and deepen, so that your life seems to be delightfully committed to a profusion of kind actions.

You cannot pass a day without meeting with opportunities for kind actions. And kind acts are as easy as they are frequent. When kindness calls for self-denial, sacrifice is noble and rewarding. You always gain more than you lose. You gain even outwardly, but the inward gain is greater. The wonderful effects of a kind deed make you wonder why you do not do more kind things.

∞

Kindness is contagious

No kind action ever stops with itself. One kind action leads to another. Good example is followed. A single act of kindness throws out roots in all directions, and the roots spring up and make new trees. The greatest work that kindness does to others is that it makes them kind themselves. The kindest men are generally those who have received the greatest number of kindnesses. As you become kinder yourself by practicing kindness, so the people you are kind to, if they were kind before, learn to be kinder, or if they were not kind before, learn how to be kind. Thus, there is no better thing you can do for others than to be kind to them. Your kindness, after the grace of God, is the greatest gift they can receive.

∞

Kindness is one of God's
greatest gifts to the world

Kindness drives gloom and darkness from souls and puts hope into fainting hearts. It sweetens sorrow and lessens pain. It discovers unsuspected beauties of human character and calls forth a response from all that is best in souls. Kindness purifies, glorifies, and ennobles all that it touches. It opens the floodgates of children's laughter and gathers the tears of repentant love. It lightens the burden of weariness.

Kindness stops the torrent of angry passion, takes the sting from failure, and kindles courageous ambition. It lifts the unfortunate, leads back the wayward, and walks in the steps of our Savior.

Kindness is too often left uncultivated because people do not sufficiently understand its value. Men may be charitable, merciful, and self-sacrificing, yet not kind. Kindness, as a grace, is not always sufficiently cultivated even among some devout people. Many devout people are unkind. There is sometimes a sort of spiritual selfishness in their devotion, which may interfere with kindness. This calls for much vigilance.

Kindness is the grand cause of God in the world. Where it is natural, it must be supernaturally planted. Your mission in life should be to reconquer for God's glory His unhappy world and give it back to Him. Devote yourself to the beautiful apostolate of kindness, so that you and others may enjoy the bliss of Divine Life.

Become a member of the *Fraternity of Kindness*. No enrollment is necessary. There are no officers, no meetings, and no dues. You must make up your mind that you want to belong to it and then begin immediately to keep the rules.

The rules are simple — three little *don'ts* and three little *dos*.

Don'ts:
1. Don't speak unkindly of anyone.
2. Don't speak unkindly to anyone.
3. Don't act unkindly toward anyone.

Dos:
1. Do speak kindly of someone at least once a day.
2. Do think kindly about someone at least once a day.
3. Do act kindly toward someone at least once a day.

For any unkindness committed:
1. Make a brief act of contrition, such as "My Jesus, mercy!"
2. Offer an apology, if possible.
3. Say a little prayer — such as "Bless N., O Lord" —
for the one to whom you have been unkind.

∞

Courtesy demonstrates love and respect

It is a duty of charity to be courteous to others. When the respect we feel toward another does not remain secret in the heart but finds outward expression, it may be called *courtesy*. St. Paul demands in no uncertain terms that we must honor our neighbor. He describes courtesy thus: "Love one another with brotherly affection; outdo one another in showing honor."[7]

Courtesy is the habit of treating other human beings with deference and respect because they are the image and likeness of God. It involves politeness, patience, thoughtfulness, helpfulness, and kindness.

Contempt hurts. People are not indifferent as to what others think or say of them. A bitter word, an insult, or mockery hurts like a slap in the face. A malicious insult may rob a man of all joy of living. Hence our Lord ranks those who insult others with murderers: "You have heard that it was said to the men of old, 'You shall not kill; and whoever kills shall be liable to judgment.' But I say to you that everyone who is angry with his brother shall be liable to judgment; whoever insults his brother shall be liable to the council, and whoever says, 'You fool!' shall be liable to the Hell of fire."[8]

[7] Rom 12:10.
[8] Matt. 5:21-22.

Respect and courtesy do good to a man. The honor that others pay us in word or deed adds to the joy of life. The expression of genuine respect on the part of our neighbor does more than do good: it meets a crying need of our nature. The respect of our fellowmen strengthens our good will and urges us to strive for ever-higher ideals.

Because man is in need of honor, all countries have devised certain forms by which we can give expression to the sentiment of respect for others. Greetings, hospitality, sympathy in joy and sorrow — the whole life of a people is regulated by this code. The law of love adopts these directions.

✆

Everyone deserves your courtesy

Love broadens the laws of courtesy. Honor should be paid not only to those above us, not only to our equals, but to "one another," as St. Paul says. No one should be excluded from the universal law of honoring one another.

Love should also deepen and spiritualize courtesy. Courtesy is supernaturalized when you remember that Christ will consider all that you have done to others as having been done to Him. A Christian sees in every man much more than just a man; he sees in him a child of God, a brother of Christ, and, in a sense, even God Himself.

St. Paul's words — "outdo one another in showing honor" — have a deeper, richer meaning than mere politeness. Respect is more than politeness. Respect reminds us of the tender, loving reverence of a child, of a disciple, or of an angel.

Let your politeness be the politeness of the heart. There is no outward token of politeness without some deep moral foundation. Love will breathe into even purely formal politeness respect, good will, and that all-embracing kindness which does not wait to be greeted, but is first with its greeting.

Courtesy is the kindness of the heart, manifested in our dealing with our fellowmen. Genuine courtesy is merely the method of being a gentleman or a gentlewoman. Cardinal Newman says, "A gentleman is one who never inflicts pain."[9]

A gentleman has his eyes on all those present; he is tender toward the bashful, gentle toward the distant, and merciful toward the absent. He guards against introducing any topics that may irritate or wound; he is seldom wearisome. He makes light of favors that he confers. He never speaks of himself, except when compelled to do so, never defends himself by heated retort, has no liking for slander or gossip, is careful not to impute wrong motives to those who interfere with him, interprets everything for the best, if he can, and, if he cannot, is silent.

A gentleman is never mean or little in his disputes, never takes unfair advantage, never mistakes personalities or sharp sayings for arguments, and never insinuates evil that he dare not say out. He observes the maxim that we should ever conduct ourselves toward an enemy as if he were one day to be our friend.

No matter on how intimate a footing you stand with someone, that intimacy should never destroy courtesy. You cannot possibly live in constant daily contact with others without noticing their faults and selfishness. Your own faults, like theirs, are bound to come to the surface.

There is one means that — perhaps more than any other — can smooth your relations with others and make them not only bearable, but, to a certain extent, pleasant, and that means is the

---

[9] John Henry Cardinal Newman, *The Idea of a University*, "Knowledge and Religious Duty."

observance of the courtesies of life — little acts of kindness and politeness.

It may easily happen that you are more polite and courteous to people outside your home or people you never expect to meet again, than to those who are members of your family or whose friendship is really worth cultivating. You may sometimes be neglectful of those whom you love, but courteous toward those for whom you care little. Consider the woman who, after scolding and scowling at her children, runs to the door when company is announced, but first smooths her ruffled temper and wreathes her face in smiles.

If you make it a point in your dealings with your fellowmen always to treat them as you would like to have them treat you, there will be no occasion for any breach of courtesy or good manners. Even a simple thank-you is important in the lives of human beings. No matter how trifling or insignificant the favor conferred may be, it merits acknowledgment, and one who is negligent in this respect deserves to be considered ill-bred and ignorant.

Learn to think of others first. Small courtesies are the perfume of life. Kindness is the art of pleasing, the knack of contributing as much as possible to the ease and happiness of those with whom you converse.

∞

Courtesy calls for dependability

Dependability, especially in little things, is an act of courtesy. There are some people who can be counted on to keep their word in any important matter, but who are untrustworthy in the small affairs of daily life. They thus become a source of annoyance to their friends. How careless they are in punctuality, in performing little services, and in remembering anniversaries.

• *Dependability is tested by punctuality.* It is a breach of courtesy to be unpunctual. A very provoking weakness of character is an inability to be on time. It can do much harm when tardiness repeatedly inconveniences others.

There are many occasions in your life when punctuality means a great deal to your friends. If you are dependable, you will be punctual and conscientious about fulfilling commitments. When you have promised to meet a friend at a certain hour in a certain place, or when you have promised to render a certain service by a given time, you are really testing your character. If you are undependable, you will often make others wait for you and permit a number of things to interfere with your promptness in fulfilling your word.

The plans and arrangements of one person are very often dependent on the word or conscientiousness of others. Complications can result from failure to keep appointments promptly, and all who are inconvenienced by the delay cannot help but form an unfavorable judgment about the one who failed.

You show discourtesy and weakness of character if you find that you are frequently making excuses to others because you put them out by not keeping appointments; if you are careless about making mental or written note of the exact time when you are expected to meet someone else; if you are easily diverted from definite obligations to others by chance meetings or conversations or passing interests; if you consider punctuality of little importance; or if you are in the habit of putting off preparations to keep appointments until it becomes impossible to be on time. Whether you are in a position of authority over others or not, whether in business or the professional or social life, you are uncharitable if you are not on time. *Mañana* may be good enough for others, but it should not be good enough for you.

• *Dependability is tested in the routine matters of charity*, little deeds of service that friends undertake to perform for one another as a matter of course in daily life, such as mailing a letter, picking up an item at the store, or giving a message to another. A dependable friend will count no favor too small to be fulfilled exactly and promptly.

• *Dependability is tested also by timely remembrances*. A dependable person will think, ahead of time, of occasions when a word or a gift or a kind deed will be especially appreciated by others. Such a person not only remembers birthdays and anniversaries, but is never too busy for a timely visit to others in times of trial. Undependable persons are usually too occupied with selfish interests to think of such opportunities.

Try to be dependable even in little things. Dependability is one of the most enviable characteristics you can possess, for it includes unselfishness, punctuality, thoughtfulness, loyalty, and charity.

∞

Your conversation must reflect courtesy

Courtesy is manifested clearly in conversation. You are a poor listener if you are solely interested in leading every conversation and showing no interest in anything that is said by others; if you are uneasy while others are speaking and are thinking only of what you are going to say when you get a chance; if you belittle the truth or value of what others say by always butting in something more significant, always topping their stories with something better; if you interrupt others in order that you may speak and reveal your pride and self-love; or if you are unable to keep silence while others are managing to keep a conversation alive.

You are a good listener if you listen gravely and with interest to others because you realize that you do not know everything and there is always something to be learned. Only the fool is so wrapped up in himself and his own ideas that he is bored with listening to others. You are a good listener if you listen as much as you talk, because thereby you want to show kindness and consideration to others. By doing so, you will give them joy, earn their confidence, and open the way to innumerable other forms of charity. As a good listener, you translate into your conduct the virtues of humility and charity. These virtues are all the greater when the conversation of others is dull or ignorant or commonplace.

It is uncharitable to ignore certain of one's companions during a conversation. This is done when, in a group of three or more persons, two of the group launch out into a personal conversation whose subject matter and interest completely exclude the other members of the group. This springs from selfishness and a sense of self-importance.

If you are guilty of such self-centered conversation, you reveal just how small you are. Charity demands, and the rules of politeness (which are charity in action) prescribe, that your personal interests be subordinated to the interests of a group. This holds for all — the famous no less than the obscure.

∞

Christ is the model of courtesy

Courtesy costs little and profits much. It is the oil without which the wheels of that mighty mechanism, human society, would soon get overheated. It eases social life with many a pleasant hour and wins for us a love that all our virtues, gifts, and merits would not secure. It also gives us an influence with others such as neither diplomacy nor violence could procure. Courtesy is one of the noblest and happiest products of the Christian philosophy of life.

In the course of the ages, there appeared only one who embodied all the characteristics of a perfect gentleman, and that was Jesus Christ. In all His career of thirty-three years, not a single instance of unkindness can be discovered. The sweetness of His smile, the glint of His eye, the sympathy that crept into His face as He consoled, comforted, or encouraged someone in need of help — all bespoke real kindness and affection for His fellowman. Even when He chided hypocrites, He was impelled by love for those whom He saw exploited.

Gentleness, respect for the feelings of others, and consideration of their circumstances are the chief qualities of a gentleman or a lady. To be gentle and courteous is to imitate Christ. Our Lord said, "Blessed are the meek, for they shall inherit the earth."[10]

∞

Charity includes a proper love of self

Charity imposes an obligation to love oneself supernaturally for God's sake. God Himself has implanted in us a tendency toward self-love which is the mainspring of all the activities of our nature. It is a law of nature to love yourself for your own sake. Your charity must include yourself, because you are loved by God.

St. Benedict Joseph Labre[11] made the following significant statement: "A Christian ought in a manner to have three hearts in

---

[10] Matt. 5:5.

[11] St. Benedict Joseph Labre (1748-1783), pilgrim to the chief shrines in western Europe who lived on alms.

one: one for God, another for his neighbor, and the third for himself. It is necessary that the first heart be for God: pure and sincere, that it direct all its actions toward Him, that it breathe only with love for Him and with ardor in His service, that it embrace all the crosses it pleases God to send. The second heart must be for our neighbor: generous, fearing no labor, no suffering in his service, compassionate, praying for the conversion of sinners, the souls in Purgatory, consoling those who are afflicted. The third heart, which is for himself, should be firm in its resolutions, abhorring all sin, mortified even to a life of sacrifices, giving its body to austerity and penance."

The natural love you have for yourself can be directed to God and be made virtuous. But even then it is not genuine charity. Your natural love of self must be conquered in deference to your love of yourself as a friend of God, as when your love of ease is made to give way to love of God's law or to the love of the poverty, humiliation, or pain that associates you more closely with Christ.

Thus, religion adds strength to the right kind of love of self because it recognizes the soul's infinite worth and divine beauty. It speaks of the nobility and destiny even of the body. No one has a deeper or a more intelligent love for himself than a Christian who lives according to the teachings of his Faith.

A well-ordered charity demands that you begin with yourself in the Mystical Body of Christ — before you are able to love all others in that body. A vast common enterprise in which we must all take part is to help each other reach the purpose for which we were created: to know, love, and serve God in this world, and to be happy with Him in Heaven.

But sometimes self-love is unwilling to remain within the boundaries assigned to it by the Creator. Instead of contenting itself with the role of a servant, self-love wishes to be its own master.

In this way, love of self turns to selfishness. It prefers its own pleasure and convenience to the interests of God and neighbors, and ends by having but one aim in all that it undertakes: self.

As a rule, selfishness is disguised so that your neighbor alone is able to recognize it. If you want to know whether you are selfish, ask the people around you. Only they can tell you whether you are inconsiderate, exacting, ambitious, or eager to have your own way. Only they can tell you whether selfishness makes you withdraw from people, whether you present a sour face to those around you, and whether you rarely utter a kind word to anyone.

It is impossible for love and selfishness to live together in your soul. Either love must overcome and finally cast out egoism, or egoism will overcome love and cast it forth, so that nothing will be left but the empty name of love and a sad self-deception. By losing charity, you lose your highest possession — the virtue by which you become like to God.

The loss of love invariably entails also the loss of many other good things. Peace disappears. The selfish man knows no rest. He feels compelled to strive for more, and then to defend and watch over his acquisitions. He is suspicious of the intentions of others, compares himself with them, and lives in anxiety. He does not feel sure even of himself. He has lost his real freedom, for he has become the slave of the evil instinct of self-love.

The voice of even a noble heart is often drowned by the voice of selfishness, which follows every human being like his own shadow. Even kind men sometimes succumb to these voices of greed, revengefulness, and ambition. The voice of passion too easily silences the voice of reason, which should guide us on the road of love. The question asked is: "Why should my advantage be subordinated to that of another? Why should I love my neighbor as myself?"

If selfishness has fettered your rightful love for yourself, do all you can to break these shackles, even if it hurts. As St. Ignatius Loyola[12] advises, "If the unmortified movements of nature make us speak or act in opposition to the principles we profess, we must chasten them with severity until they obey us." Make some sacrifice each day in order to render a service to another. Each sacrifice will help to restore freedom to true charity.

∞

Make others feel important

If you want to make friends, go out of your way to do things for other people — things that require time, energy, unselfishness, and thoughtfulness. Greet people enthusiastically and sincerely. A man's name is to him the most important sound in his language. One of the simplest ways of gaining good will is by remembering names and making people feel important. Take the time and energy necessary to concentrate and fix names indelibly in your mind.

Make other people feel important, and do it sincerely. If you are so selfish that you cannot radiate a little happiness and pass on a bit of honest appreciation without trying to get something out of the other person in return, you will meet with failure. The only return you should try to get out of someone is the feeling that you have done a favor for him without his being able to do anything whatever in return for you. That is a feeling that lingers in your memory long after the incident has passed.

There is a law that, if obeyed, will bring you countless friends and constant happiness. Jesus taught it centuries ago and summed

---

[12] St. Ignatius Loyola (1491-1556), founder of the Society of Jesus.

it up in one sentence: "Do unto others as you would have others do unto you."[13] You want the approval of those with whom you come in contact. You want recognition of your true worth. You do not want to listen to cheap, insincere flattery, but you crave sincere appreciation. So obey the Golden Rule, and do for others what you would have others do for you — always and everywhere.

∞

A supernatural motive increases the benefits of selflessness

In all fairness to yourself, you ought to be more alert and humanly practical in dealing with your fellowmen. On the merely natural plane, your own good is advanced through the good you do to others. How much greater benefits will come to you by lifting these natural tendencies to the supernatural plane!

Selfishness often darkens the vision and restrains the hand stretched forth to do a kindness. Do not be one of those who, for the sake of honor or praise from people, are ready to make great sacrifices, but neglect the little acts of kindness that add more luster to their name than do great deeds inspired by selfish motives. A kind word or a kind act is like lighting another man's candle with your own, which loses none of its brightness by what the other gains.

Charity should be wholehearted and sympathetic, for the manner of giving is worth more than the gift itself. Love makes you ready to anticipate even the least of your neighbor's wishes and to render him all possible service.

The tendency to be self-centered is strong in most of us. This is why St. Francis de Sales[14] states, "Our principal business should be

---

[13] Cf. Matt. 7:12; Luke 6:31.

[14] St. Francis de Sales (1567-1622), Bishop of Geneva.

to conquer ourselves, and to become more perfect every day in this practice. It is particularly necessary that we should apply ourselves to be victorious in little temptations, such as boastfulness, suspicion, jealousy, indolence, and vanity. By so doing, we shall obtain the strength to resist greater ones."

Check up on yourself regarding your own self-centeredness, which shows itself in self-satisfaction, the seeking of personal advantages, or a low opinion of others. Perhaps you let self get in your way entirely too frequently. Try to "get out of yourself": rid yourself of gloomy obsession; stop brooding over hurt feelings and apparent wrongs. Instead, make every effort to foster cheerful thoughts, to look at the miseries of others in life and see them through their eyes, and to cultivate a tender helpfulness toward them. In general, try to exercise the charity upon them that you would so much appreciate, if it were bestowed upon you.

To do good to others in the hope that, in turn, our Lord will be good to you is a supernatural motive, even if it is self-centered. To do good to others with the consciousness that Christ asks it of you is less egoistic. To do good to others because you are convinced that Christ will consider it as having been done to Him personally is a sign of pure love of God. To do good to others because thereby you can please God, and you want to give Him the best you can, is perfect love of God.

Do all the good to others that circumstances allow. If you concentrate on yourself too often, your life will be flat and empty. Lively interest in others makes you rise above the pettiness of self-love. Self-love is to be dissolved in the crucible of a common interest in people. Self-effacement in order that others may be made happy is a lifework that will be most richly rewarded by God. It is Christlike to give generously of your kind thoughts, your heartening words, and your kind deeds.

In order to have true love, you must have the faith that Christ Himself gave to the world, the religion of love, which teaches us to love man for the sake of God even at the cost of sacrifice. In spite of the opposition of your passions, your faith urges you to advance in charity. St. Peter expresses it in these words: "For this very reason, make every effort to supplement your faith with virtue, and virtue with knowledge, and knowledge with self-control, and self-control with steadfastness, and steadfastness with godliness, and godliness with brotherly affection, and brotherly affection with love."[15]

And St. Paul says, "I appeal to you therefore, brethren, by the mercies of God, to present your bodies as a living sacrifice, holy and acceptable to God, which is your spiritual worship."[16] Thus your every task, even the most commonplace, can be changed, as the water was at Cana, into the wine of sacrifice.[17]

∞

Master your senses and passions through discipline

Look for happiness not in selfishness, but in self-denial. The Son of God preached self-denial to spur us on the way to happiness. "Do not think that I have come to bring peace on earth; I have not come to bring peace, but a sword."[18] He meant that He had come to wage war against self and selfish passions. He came to free men from the misery into which their selfishness had led them.

Love calls for generosity and self-sacrifice. Love is the heart and soul of religion. Love is not content with fair words but seeks

[15] 2 Pet. 1:5-7.
[16] Rom. 12:1.
[17] Cf. John 2:9.
[18] Matt. 10:34.

to assert itself by deeds. Without practicing self-sacrifice, you are pleasing only to yourself.

The Holy Spirit sanctifies souls through the gift of grace and inspires souls to great generosity in the service of God and their neighbor. His grace gave to the martyrs courage to die for the Faith and to the saints the fortitude to lead holy lives and perform heroic deeds of virtue.

In this life, sacrifice must be joined to love. The love of God cannot be practical if we do not renounce inordinate self-love — that is, the threefold concupiscence of the flesh, the eyes, and the pride of life.[19]

Passions are selfish and blind in themselves. They need direction. If left to choose its own course, a passion can easily become like an insane driver at the wheel of a high-powered automobile. Discipline is necessary if you wish to have order in your life. Your passions and emotions should be under the control of your reason, enlightened by faith, and your reason and intelligence should be under the control of God. If one of the passions gets out of line, your reason, operating through the power of the will, aided by grace, must put it in its proper place. Otherwise, the passion will dominate you.

St. Vincent de Paul[20] gives us this advice: "He who would advance in perfection should take particular care not to allow his passions to govern him, which will destroy with one hand the edifice he builds with the other. To be master of one's self, it is necessary to begin early to resist our inclinations; for if once [they are] deeply rooted and strengthened, there is hardly ever a remedy."

---

[19] Cf. 1 John 2:16.

[20] St. Vincent de Paul (c. 1580-1660), founder of the Lazarist Fathers and the Sisters of Charity.

Sensuality, or love of the senses, is a foe of love. It frequently kills true love, because sensuality is simply self-love. Sensuality proceeds from the body. No bodily sense ever gives anything; it can only take and appropriate. Of all the passions, sensuality is the most violent in its desires and the most reckless in its taking of the object on which it has set its heart. Even though its speech and conduct still assume the airs of love, its effects may become those of hate.

St. Jude says, "It is these who set up divisions, worldly people, devoid of the Spirit."[21] The sensual person is devoid of the Spirit of God, the spirit of genuine, unselfish love. But the slave of sensuality is not always aware of the true nature of his disease. Sensuality robs love of its great and noble strength, which bestows and achieves great things without a thought of self and remains true to the end.

Your love for your neighbor must be spiritualized if it is to be faithful. If your love is mingled with sensuality, you shall have to deny yourself constantly everything toward which sensuality urges you. Love must grow ever more pure until it does not find its goal in the flesh. Even conjugal love, which, in accordance with its very nature and purpose, may be a sensual love, should become more spiritual, so that those who become "one flesh"[22] may end up becoming "one heart and soul."[23]

The passions and feelings and emotions in themselves are good and worthwhile servants. When they are allowed to get out of line, they are capable of evil. The greatest evil of all results when the human intelligence rebels against God. This is the sin of pride.

[21] Jude 1:19.
[22] Gen. 2:24.
[23] Acts 4:32.

An important part in achieving perfect self-control consists in discovering and admitting your predominant fault. Once you have done this, your efforts will be concentrated, and you stand a much better chance of success against your enemy.

∞

Self-denial brings peace and happiness

Peace based on surrender to our passions is what the world gives, but the peace Jesus gives is founded on victory over our passions. The peace offered by the world is a source of unhappiness; the peace Jesus offers is a source of true joy. The Master said, "He who finds his life will lose it, and he who loses his life for my sake will find it."[24] He meant that he who seeks himself instead of God finds unhappiness and death.

Our Lord said, "If any man would come after me, let him deny himself and take up his cross and follow me."[25] You are not asked to love sacrifice for its own sake. It is enough if you love it for God's sake. Here on earth you cannot love God without renouncing whatever is an obstacle to His love. Then sacrifice becomes first tolerable, and soon even acceptable. When you accept for the sake of God the sacrifices He demands, you have not only the hope, but the certainty, of pleasing Him, of giving Him glory, and of working out the salvation of your soul. No labors are too great for a loving heart, for where there is love, there is no labor. With God's grace, this labor of love opens the door for cheerfulness in the service of God.

If you are looking for happiness, you must be ready to walk the path of self-denial. You can find happiness only by resisting the

---

[24] Matt. 10:39.
[25] Matt. 16:24; Mark 8:34; Luke 9:23.

unruly inclinations of your passions, not by serving them. The more complete your detachment from the things of this world, the happier you will be. Even good Christians become uneasy, anxious, and disappointed as a result of a lack of self-denial. They are struggling with their attachments to the passing temporal things that attract them, while God at the same time seeks to draw them to Himself.

Happiness, therefore, consists in renunciation of self, of one's own mind and will, to listen to God and to do His holy will, to serve Him either in Himself or in the creatures representing Him. Happiness consists in rising above self and creatures to attach oneself, mind and heart, to God, the Source of all goodness and happiness.

St. Teresa[26] said, "I have never known real sorrow from the day I decided to serve with all my power my Lord and divine Consoler." One of her spiritual daughters, St. Thérèse of the Child Jesus,[27] wrote, "From the moment I began to forget myself, I led the happiest life possible." St. John Vianney[28] said, "We must ask for the love of crosses, and then they become sweet. I experienced this myself. I have been slandered. I have had crosses. I have had almost more than I could bear. I began to ask for the love of crosses; then I was happy. I said to myself, 'Therein alone is found peace, happiness.'"

The saints were saints because they were cheerful when it was difficult to be cheerful, patient when it was difficult to be patient, silent when they wanted to speak, and agreeable when they felt an

---

[26] St. Teresa of Avila (1515-1582), Carmelite nun and mystic.

[27] St. Thérèse of Lisieux (1873-1897), Carmelite nun.

[28] St. John Vianney (1786-1859), patron saint of parish priests; known as the Curé d'Ars.

urge to scream. They pushed forward when they wanted to stand still. *Sainthood* is simply another word for self-forgetfulness and generosity.

Sacrifice is difficult. But you will develop strength in sacrifice if you are fully resolved to refuse God nothing, if you cheerfully accept disappointments and crosses, if you mortify your passions, if you thank God for the crosses He sends you, and if you pray for a spirit of sacrifice.

Your soul can find rest only in God because you have been created for God. Created objects that you love give joy only in the measure in which you love them in God, who is their Author. They become bitter when you love them apart from Him.

Worldlings make the mistake of placing their happiness in following their own wills and in satisfying all their passions. This road leads to bitterness, sadness, and even to despair. They seek for happiness in themselves and in other creatures, but they have been able to grasp only an empty and passing share of it.

Ask God for the grace to love the Cross. In spite of your natural aversion to it, earnestly resolve to forget yourself completely so as to think only of the interests of God and of souls. Try to find happiness in bringing happiness to others.

∞

Imitate Christ's self-sacrifice

Our Lord's love for us is the model of self-sacrificing love for our neighbor. He said, "This is my commandment, that you love one another as I have loved you. Greater love has no man than this, that a man lay down his life for his friends. You are my friends if you do what I command you."[29]

[29] John 15:12-14.

The imitation of Christ is the highest type of virtue. Christ walked in love among us for thirty-three years and "went about doing good."[30] He offered Himself willingly and lovingly, not under compulsion, in order to secure our welfare. "Christ loved us and gave Himself up for us, a fragrant offering and sacrifice to God."[31] Christ's sacrifice destroyed the evil order of sin. The Father was pleased with the fragrant incense of the oblation of Calvary. There is no limitation to our Lord's love for us. To die, if necessary, for those we love, is the greatest proof of love, and Jesus gave His life for us.

How often are you willing to inconvenience yourself or make a sacrifice for your neighbor, much less lay down your life for him? You are not always required to give your life for another, but you must always live for others. The true meaning of charity is more the giving of what you *are* than of what you *have*. Your neighbor does not require a portion of your money or possessions, but he longs for a portion of your heart. Love cannot exist unless it is based upon the gift of self that is self-sacrifice. St. Paul says, "Each one must do as he has made up his mind, not reluctantly or under compulsion, for God loves a cheerful giver."[32]

Because the sacrifice of Christ was so pleasing to God, He gladly accepts any offering or sacrifice on your part that you unite with it. Place upon the altar at Holy Mass the pains and sacrifices that human contacts demand of you, and make of them an expiatory offering in union with Christ. "As Christ loves us," you should be ready to sacrifice yourself for your neighbor, be it for the salvation of his soul or for the welfare of his temporal concern.

[30] Acts 10:38.
[31] Eph. 5:2.
[32] 2 Cor. 9:7.

You need grace in order to imitate God. You can have it for the asking, if you really desire to be like Christ. Plead for the grace to recognize where you can imitate His conduct.

∞

Yield to others when it is called for

St. Paul advises us to adapt ourselves to the ways of others: "Give no offense to Jews or to Greeks or to the Church of God, just as I try to please all men in everything I do, not seeking my own advantage, but that of many, that they may be saved."[33] St. Paul encourages us in these words: "Rejoice with those who rejoice; weep with those who weep. Live in harmony with one another."[34] In the midst of his continual journeys, he labored with his own hands so as not to be a burden to the Christian communities who received him.[35] All these acts sprang from the same source: Christ seen through faith in his neighbor.

St. Paul adapted himself to others insofar as the spirit of Christ permitted it. He renounced personal rights and liberties so that he might gain new followers for Christ. This is true apostolic zeal and disinterested charity.

One way of getting along with people is the ability to give in. Strength of character means the ability to give in to others from motives of love, kindness, and humility, and to do so gracefully, when no sin is involved. It also means the ability to stand on principle, and not to give in, when sin is involved.

One of the clearest tests of character is to examine your conscience on the manner in which you give in to the ideas, the plans,

[33] 1 Cor. 10:32-33.
[34] Rom. 12:15-16.
[35] 2 Cor. 12:16.

and the desires of others. You show weakness of character if you are unable to give in gracefully or at all when there is reason for giving in. It is also a sign of the weakness of character if you are too ready to give in, even when sound principles are at stake. There are people who will not give in when nothing is at stake, but who will almost always give in when virtue and right principles are at stake.

You express your *unwillingness to give in* if you refuse to associate with persons who are not willing to let you have your way in all disputes over plans and issues; if you insist on your viewpoint at all costs so that in arguments with others you become louder and louder as the argument goes on; if you pout and show resentment, sometimes for a long time, when forced against your will to give in to somebody else; or if you are overbearing with your family and friends and answer only with scorn to objections they raise against your ideas or your plans.

You express *too much readiness to give in*, even when sound principles are at stake, if you are quick to follow along when somebody suggests doing something morally off-color, such as reading a questionable magazine; if you readily join with others in evil conversation because you do not want them to think you are prudish or ignorant of evil; if you agree with another's criticism of persons you do not like in order to get even with them or bring them down to your level; or if you go along with someone who has power to advance you, even though that person's reputation is not good.

When another's good is at stake, do not shirk a little inconvenience, or lament over foregoing a personal privilege, or argue over a slight disadvantage, or fear that your reputation will be affected. Putting self in the background is a good renunciation for human nature. Putting the needs and interests of others ahead of your own, for the love of God, will benefit people more than you will ever be able to estimate in this world. Your intentions will be pleasing to God, and someone, somewhere, somehow will be benefitted in God's own good time. You yourself will be doing much good, strengthening your soul by the exercise of virtue and meriting an eternal reward. You should be glad to make these sacrifices for the love of God. Like Paul, you will be adapting yourself to all, for the love of God.

∞

Make little sacrifices for others

St. Paul advises the sacrifice of little freedoms for the sake of others. He would even enslave himself in order to save souls for Christ. His language explains his fervent zeal for the salvation of souls: "For though I am free from all men, I have made myself a slave to all, that I might win the more. . . . To the weak I became weak, that I might win the weak. I have become all things to all men, that I might by all means save some."[36]

In your case, enslavement would imply the voluntary deprivation of those little freedoms that are so sweet to you. This might mean being very attentive to the needs and wants of others: saving them steps, lightening their burdens, giving them new hope and courage, offering them the heartening clasp of the hand, or performing a favor asked at a time inconvenient to you.

These personal denials and the self-restraints involved in them are very pleasing to God. These little courtesies in daily contacts done supernaturally are little in themselves, yet significant of the spirit of Christ to those whom they benefit. Try to perform these attentions with such ease and interest that the recipient may feel honored. You have accomplished much if he lives a more holy life in consequence of your kindness toward him.

[36] 1 Cor. 9:19, 22.

Endeavor to be more strongly intent on doing good to others for their eternal welfare than base passion can be to get followers of ignoble causes. Exercise at least an equal zeal to win souls for Christ.

∞

Sacrifice helps you win souls for Christ

St. Paul advises spiritual self-denial. He is ready to give his very life-substance for the welfare of souls. The peak of selflessness in the exercise of charity is presented in these words: "My little children . . . I am again in travail until Christ be formed in you!"[37] Here we see a beautiful blend of maternal tenderness and paternal strength. He calls his apostolic zeal the suffering of the pangs of spiritual childbirth for souls. The anxieties, sufferings, and fears for their welfare and loyalty to Christ constituted a childbirth of a spiritual nature. He is suffering the pangs of childbirth for the Galatians a second time. His first "labor" was bringing them into the Church. But they had become perverted. Hence, great anxiety arose in him that "Christ be formed" in them once more.

Soul-pain is the price of conversions. No sin can be blotted out except by the soul-pain we know as supernatural contrition. If you want to win souls for Christ, you must be willing to endure the anguish for sin that sinners do not experience, in order to win at least ultimately the grace of repentance for them. You may have to go through the agonies of delayed hopes for many hearts, and even seeming failure at the end, for someone whose soul has been your deep concern. But your sincere devotion to bring a soul to Christ will not be in vain. God knows the secret workings of His grace in souls.

[37] Gal. 4:19.

The spirit of St. Paul is to put yourself even to the greatest sacrifice that others may be blessed. This is spiritual greatness. You should have at least so much generosity as to forego personal advantages voluntarily so that others may be brought closer to Christ. The essence of Christianity is to be found in selfless service bestowed upon your neighbor for the love of God. Heroic charity is possible only where true love of God has taken hold of the soul. The more deeply you become imbued with the spirit of Christ, the more selfless you become. The more generous you strive to be, so much the more have you to give to others. The greater your love for Christ, the holier and more effective will be your love for your neighbor.

Ask our Lord frequently to prompt you strongly to make sacrifices for the interests of others, especially when you are blind to the situations or are reluctant to see them. He knew as no one else does what enslavement in the name of charity entails. Ask for the grace to become more like Him in sacrificing yourself for others. Ask your heavenly Mother, who "went with haste into the hill country"[38] to serve her cousin Elizabeth, that you may learn true selflessness.

Your love for souls must be supernatural and truly apostolic. Selfish concern and sentimental affection must be avoided. You must buoy up your courage with Jesus in the ordeal of sacrificing yourself, and trust to the union of your prayer with His for the graces you implore for souls. Learn something of St. Paul's spirit of holy disinterestedness, so that his words may also be true of you: "Brethren, my heart's desire and prayer to God for them is that they may be saved."[39]

[38] Luke 1:39.
[39] Rom. 10:1.

The apostolate of prayer, sacrifice, and penance for the salvation of souls is open to all. It is not confined to those who have direct contact with them. Many an individual outside of the ranks of the priesthood of the Church has been mother to a soul of another. The invalid confined to a bed of suffering, as well as the cloistered nun in her solitude of prayer, may exercise a most active apostolate in saving souls. Saintly souls in the solitude of their communings with God or in the faithful accomplishment of their daily duties may contribute as much to the conversion of sinners as missionaries who deal directly with souls. St. Thérèse of the Child Jesus said: "Jesus desires that the salvation of souls should be achieved by our sacrifices and our love. Let us offer our sufferings to Jesus to save them. Let us live for them; let us be apostles."

∞

Radiate cheerfulness

Cheerfulness is a very great help in fostering the virtue of charity. Cheerfulness itself is a virtue. Therefore, it is a habit that can and should be acquired.

Cheerfulness is perhaps best represented in the word *affability*. St. Thomas Aquinas[40] places affability under the general heading of the cardinal virtue of justice, the virtue that prompts us to give to others what is their due under any sense of duty or obligation. You are obliged to help and not hinder others around you in the world on their way toward Heaven. Not only are you to help the needy by your alms, and the erring by your advice, but you are also to help all whom you know or meet by your kindliness, pleasantness, and affability of manner.

---

[40] St. Thomas Aquinas (c. 1225-1274), Dominican philosopher and theologian.

Cheerfulness of attitude and manner is a great help to those who come into contact with you. If you are a sour, unsociable, gloomy-looking person, you will make people feel uneasy, and you will intensify your own temptations to give way to sadness. On the other hand, if you are cheerful, you will lift the spirits of people, invite their confidence, and increase their hope of serving God well.

If you consistently present a gloomy attitude toward life and everybody around you, it may be because you are suffering from a case of self-pity. You let your sorrows and misfortunes overwhelm you. Or you may be prompted by envy to refuse even an effort at being cheerful because you are thinking of the many good things others have that you are denied. Or you may be a victim of your feelings. Temperamentally you may be inclined toward sadness, and you take the position that you should let your temperament rule you.

∞

Avoid false cheerfulness

You are not really cheerful when you lack seriousness when it is time to be serious, so that you cannot give serious attention to the important duties of life. It is dangerous and misguided cheerfulness to make light of your serious sins, to avoid all thoughts of judgment and Hell, and to be giddy and distracting to others in church or on other serious occasions. You are not really cheerful when you lack sympathy. It is a great defect of cheerfulness in your character if you cannot sympathize with the sorrows of people, if you avoid people who are suffering, or if you manifest by your attitude that you are not going to permit yourself to be disturbed by their sorrows.

You need not express your cheerfulness by smiles and laughter or jokes and light-minded chatter. In the presence of sorrow, you can adopt a serious mien and show signs of sympathy, but at the

39

same time you can express your cheerfulness in the solid motives for hope, fortitude, and patience that God has provided for all whom He asks to suffer. You will not refuse to permit any of your friends to face facts that are a cause of sorrow, nor will you try to think up exaggerated reasons for not grieving or making light of the grieving of others.

You are not really cheerful if you are cheerful only at times, but at other times give way to sadness and melancholy. This would indicate that you are ruled entirely by your feelings. It would be even worse if you had the habit of being cheerful in the presence of some of your relatives and friends, but gloomy in the presence of others, especially your own family. You cannot afford to have one attitude toward your family and another toward those with whom you mingle outside your home.

You must learn to rise above your feelings, even though the control of feelings is most difficult. There is no hypocrisy in being ruled by the will rather than by the feelings. Try to live up to the ideal of being always the same toward everyone: kindly, affable, sympathetic, encouraging — in a word, cheerful. This ideal will be recognized by all, and you will spread the sunshine of joy around you.

You are not really cheerful if you must depend on dangerous stimulants of one kind or another. Drink is often an escape from reality and makes people boisterous, foolish, and degraded.

There are three important virtues that make people cheerful in the true sense of the word: hope, fortitude, and fraternal charity.

∞

Cheerfulness is founded on hope

Hope is the virtue by which you keep your eyes fixed on Heaven as the goal of your life, made certainly attainable by the merits and promises and fidelity of Jesus Christ. Since you always have something wonderful to look forward to, you are cheerful. Hope is a supernatural virtue infused at Baptism, but it requires effort and repeated actions to become effective.

You cannot be cheerful if you succumb to the vices opposed to hope, such as despair, which is a surrender to the thought that Heaven cannot be attained and that the sufferings of Hell are inevitable. St. Thérèse of the Child Jesus used to say, "We can never have too much confidence in the good God. He is so mighty, so merciful."

Worldliness urges people to capture every possible delight here and now. It leads to sadness, because there are no delights in this world that can fully satisfy the human heart. Worldliness also leads to envy, avarice, impurity, and all such causes of sadness.

∞

Fortitude allows you
to face the sorrows of life

Fortitude is a basis for cheerfulness. Fortitude induces you to face the inevitable sorrows of life and, above all, death itself, in the service of God with courage and patience. You will look to the sufferings of Christ for inspiration. You will look to the happiness of Heaven with a heart full of hope, and you will count even the greatest sufferings as a small price to pay for that reward. Therefore, try to overcome cowardice, self-pity, and lack of confidence in the goodness of God — faults that prevent you from being cheerful. As a result of these faults, you may find yourself constantly grumbling against God and everybody around you because of the sufferings you have to endure.

Do not take yourself too seriously. You have to learn not to be dismayed at making mistakes. No human being can avoid failures.

The important thing is not to let your mistakes and failures gnaw away at you. Regret is an appalling waste of energy. You cannot build on it.

Instead of wasting priceless time and energy in regret or self-reproach, the wise thing is for you to swing into action once more. People give little sympathy to those who feel sorry for themselves. If you experience misfortune, other people will not usually harden their hearts toward you. They have responsibilities to face, tasks to be done, and pleasures to be enjoyed. They expect you to take your troubles in stride and to rebound into the daily round of living. Such expectations are sensible.

When you go forward to grapple with your problems courageously and hopefully, you cannot help having a beneficial influence upon other people. Courage and hope are contagious. Spread these virtues among the persons whom you encounter; you will be rendering them and yourself an inestimable service.

∞

Doing good brings joy

By the virtue of charity for the love of God, you love and want to help all your neighbors, especially those whose lives are in some way associated with your own. One way of helping others is by an attitude of cheerfulness.

Joy is the reward of charity. This intimate joy of the soul is distinguished from all other joys by its purity. The joy that is the fruit of charity is abiding. All earthly happiness exhausts itself, except the happiness of a loving heart that knows how to share the joys and sorrows of others. The joy born of charity is one of the few joys that support you at the hour of death.

In the hour of farewell, the divine Master declared that He desired His joy to be in His disciples: "These things I have spoken to you, that my joy may be in you, and that your joy may be full."[41] Thus your joy at doing good springs from the fountain of Him who is the essence of all love, from the fountain of God. From the waters of joy that flow in the heart of God, fountains of joy will spring up in your heart if you strive to imitate God's great love in at least a small measure, like the fountains of which our Lord speaks: "The water that I shall give him will become in him a spring of water welling up to eternal life."[42]

If your heart thirsts for joy, do good to others. You will satisfy your thirst in the fountain of God's own bliss. You can find your happiness only in possessing God. St. Augustine says, "Our hearts were made for Thee, O Lord, and they are restless until they rest in Thee."[43] You can find happiness in making other people happy if your efforts are motivated by a sincere love of God.

∞

Action fosters cheer

Action is one of the most effective forms of self-encouragement and good cheer. There is something intrinsically humble about action. When you act, you come to grips with reality. Action does not make your problems magically disappear, but unlike talk or dreams or merely good resolutions, it does begin to solve them. As long as you act, there is limitless hope for you and very little room for gloominess.

In your action, however, try to take a long-range view of things. This will further serve to encourage you. You are often too

[41] John 15:11.

[42] John 4:14.

[43] St. Augustine (354-430; Bishop of Hippo), *Confessions*, Bk. 1, ch. 1.

impatient. You want quick and easy solutions. When they are not forthcoming, you get depressed. Nature has a way of taking its own sweet time, and you are part of nature. You cannot force things. Cultivate a respect for time and the essential role it plays in all human activity.

∞

Have a sense of humor

An almost indispensable aid to cheerfulness is the cultivation of a sense of humor. This does not mean being witty or being able to tell humorous stories and to make people laugh. A sense of humor is the acquired ability to see contrasts and inconsistencies in life, especially in your own life, and to be amused by them.

Without a sense of humor, you may be constantly sad over your lack of many material comforts. But a sense of humor will keep you from taking this passing world too seriously, because you will see how foolish such sadness is in the light of the truth that you have an immortal soul destined one day to enjoy the riches of Heaven. It will help you to inject this same amusement over the inconsistencies in your own life into your conversation with others, so that they, too, will be enabled at times to smile when they feel like weeping.

∞

A smile can do much good

A smile is one of nature's best means of making people happy. One of the most delightful factors in a personality is a real heartwarming smile that comes from within. Actions speak louder than words, and a smile says, "I like you. You make me happy. I am glad to see you." If you do not feel like smiling, smile anyway; make yourself smile.

A smile costs nothing, but creates much. It enriches those who receive it and does not impoverish you in the least. A smile creates happiness in the home and fosters good will among men. It is rest to the weary, daylight to the discouraged, sunshine to the sad, and nature's best remedy for trouble.

A smile is no earthly good to anyone until it is given away. None of us are so rich that we can get along without it, and none of us are really poor as long as we can smile. Nobody needs a smile so much as the one who has none to give. So get used to smiling heart-warming smiles, and you will spread sunshine in a sometimes dreary world. This sunshine is the sunshine of God's love, if you smile from the motive of loving your neighbor and making him happy for the sake of God.

Become a member of the *Apostolate of Smiling*. Your smile has work to do for God, because it is an instrument for winning souls. Sanctifying grace, dwelling in your soul, will sweeten your smile and will enable it to do much good.

Smile to yourself until you notice that your seriousness, or even severity, has vanished — until you have warmed your own heart with the development of a cheery disposition. Then go out and radiate your smile.

With a smile, you can bring new life and hope and courage into the hearts of the weary, the overburdened, the discouraged, the tempted, and the despairing. Your smile can prepare the way for a sinner's return to God. It can promote contentment, joy, satisfaction, encouragement, and confidence in the hearts of others.

Let all enjoy the beauty and inspiring cheer of your smiling face. Above all, smile at God in loving acceptance of whatever He sends into your life, and you will deserve to have the radiantly smiling face of Christ gaze on you with special love throughout eternity.

Chapter Two

Avoid passing judgment on others

If there were true charity in your heart, you would be glad to see good in your neighbor and to think well of him. Faultfinding indicates narrowness of mind. The ability to find fault is believed by some people to be a sure sign of wisdom, but nothing requires so little intelligence. Nothing is easier than faultfinding. No talent, no character, no self-denial, and no brains are required to set up this grumbling business.

A critic usually is a person who is unable to do the thing the way he thinks it should be done by others. He forgets that criticism and faultfinding, like charity, should begin at home, that is, with oneself. Added to the ignorance of the critic you will find its companion, pride, and also a sort of envy or jealousy, for the faultfinder recognizes his own inability or failure.

∞

Be patient with your superiors

Superiors are often the objects of faultfinding. Submission to authority in some way is a necessary duty of every human creature. No one can escape obedience. This is the plan God set up for the world, that He would delegate His divine authority to parents and other legitimate human superiors. He Himself gave an outstanding example of submission to that authority, for St. Luke says He "was obedient to them,"[44] meaning His mother and foster-father in the natural order of things.

Faults and defects are bound to appear in human instruments; hence, faults are to be found in superiors. A position of authority can sometimes bring into prominence the faults of human nature. Superiors, even with the best of intentions, will manifest certain defects. For instance, a superior can be the overbearing type, too obviously conscious of his position, easily aroused to impatience and anger, indifferent to the needs and complaints of those subject to them, and too insistent on trivialities. Some of these faults will inevitably produce a certain amount of irritation and friction.

God does not will the faults of superiors, but He does want you to be kind in judging them. He set up His plan of delegated authority knowing that faults would be found. In a sense, He uses those faults, and He desires those who are under authority to be purified by them. Superiors have an obligation to work against their faults, especially because of the consequences of their failure to do so.

To supernaturalize your obedience is to see God's Providence even in the faults of your superiors, and to practice devotion to duty and charity and patience in spite of these faults.

∞

Recall your own faults

Faults in others would not be so noticeable if you took time to examine your own. Borrow your neighbor's glasses sometime. See yourself as others see you, and then you may not believe all you

---

[44] Luke 2:51.

see. You seldom measure the faults of your fellowman and your own with the same rule or weigh them on the same scales. We all have one basket hanging before us in which we put our neighbor's faults, and another behind us — which we cannot see — in which we stow away our own.

St. Paul says, "Love rejoiceth not in iniquity, but rejoiceth with the truth."[45] If, when you charged a person with his faults, you credited him with his virtues too, you would probably like everybody. It is just as easy to think kindly of your neighbor as to find fault with him — even though you may not get much satisfaction out of such thoughts.

St. Thérèse of the Child Jesus wrote in her autobiography, "If, when I desire to increase in my heart love of my neighbor, the demon tries to set before my eyes the faults of one or other of the Sisters, I hasten to call to mind her virtues, her good desires; I say to myself that, if I have seen her fall once, she may well have won many victories which she conceals through humility; and that even what appears to me a fault may in truth be an act of virtue by reason of the intention."

Grace is really much more common even in the worst of men than your critical nature is generally willing to admit. You would be wise, therefore, to call in supernatural considerations to make your criticism charitable. These supernatural motives may at times depress your own ideas of yourself, but they will also encourage you to have faith in your fellowman.

Practice self-control, and refrain from criticizing your neighbor in thought and word. Do not judge your neighbor's faults. You are apt to exaggerate the faults of others, especially of those toward whom you feel a natural aversion. Instead of noticing the evil that

[45] Cf. 1 Cor. 13:6 (Douay-Rheims edition).

is found in the world, develop the habit of thinking about the good and encouraging it. You will then have a contented life.

∞

Avoid making rash judgments

You commit the sin of rash judgment when, without sufficient reason, you believe something that is harmful to another's character. Rash judgment differs from suspicion. Suspicion is a disposition of mind that causes you to think that a morally undesirable thing probably exists in another, while you still hesitate to pronounce a definite opinion regarding it.

Rash judgment is a sin against justice. Others have a right to retain the good esteem we have of them until they forfeit this right by actions unmistakably bad. Rash judgment is an act of injustice against your neighbor, for you condemn him without a hearing and without knowing the reasons and motives for his actions. You may even be under the influence of prejudice or anger. When serious injustice is done to a neighbor by rash judgment, the sin is serious.

Charity and honesty are the necessary qualities of fair judgment. Correct judgment can scarcely be expected of you. The fundamental springs of action in your own life frequently escape you and are often very secretly concealed from you through pride. If you feel an aversion to a person — that is, an unexplainable feeling of dislike or distaste for him — it is the most dangerous time for a proper opinion of him, his character, or his actions. Any judgment you pass upon him at such a time is bound to be unfair. You must be kindly disposed toward a person in order to reach a fair decision. Moods and temper and momentary feelings will influence judgments. What you look at from one angle today, you will study from another angle tomorrow, and both angles may be different from yesterday's.

∞

You cannot judge accurately from outward appearances

There are some things that you simply cannot know about a person whom you are inclined to criticize. First, you cannot know the actual condition of his mind. He may have been mentally irresponsible at the time he did the things you criticize.

Second, you cannot know his full educational and environmental background. On Judgment Day, it may be seen that his parents or teachers or friends were responsible, by neglect or wrong training or external influence, for the actions or traits that seem so blameworthy.

Third, you cannot know the actual motives behind his actions. Often you attribute motives to certain actions that would have been yours in the same circumstances. But no two human beings are exactly alike. You have probably made serious mistakes in attempting to decide the motives of others.

Fourth, you cannot know the exact degree of guilt incurred by a man for any sin. This is God's field of judgment.

You have no right to pass judgment on anybody or anything until you have examined the subject from all points of view and carefully weighed all accidental circumstances that, by their nature, might cast a different light upon the matter. To estimate a man's character truly and fairly, you would have to know all the forces of heredity in which he was brought up and in which he now lives, the stress of his passions, the limitation of his intelligence, and even his physical condition.

Natural proneness to judge others by ourselves is a weakness of our fallen nature. You decide that a certain person is impolite, another is self-centered, selfish, and unsympathetic, and another is arrogant, unfair, untrustworthy, and pleasure-loving. You arrive at such conclusions by reflex judgment. You know situations so well from personal experience that you conclude immediately that others have acted as you have done. At once you brand others with unworthy motives and sinful deeds.

Everyone who comes within the reach of your knowledge is, as it were, on trial in your mind. It is easy to be an unjust, ignorant, and even a merciless judge. The real character of the actions of others depends in great measure on the motives that prompt them, and these motives are unknown to you.

St. Ignatius Loyola says, "A judge ought not to believe an accuser until after he has heard the accused and found him to be guilty." You have no right to judge another until you have given him a chance to defend himself. To judge rashly is nothing less than to take to yourself the rights of Christ, who alone is the Supreme Judge of the living and the dead. St. Paul says, "Do not pronounce judgment before the time, before the Lord comes, who will bring to light the things now hidden in darkness and will disclose the purposes of the heart. Then every man will receive his commendation from God."[46]

You cannot judge a man by his failures; you must judge him by what he makes of them. A man's inner greatness is often tested not by what he does when the public gaze is fixed upon him, but by what he does quietly and steadily. One of the greatest lessons to learn is the knack of extracting victory out of defeat. No one is a failure who is upright and true. There is but one real failure, and that is the person who is not true to the best that is in him.

You will probably not escape being judged rashly and falsely by others sometime in life. Our Lord did not escape it; neither did the saints. It is prudent to do all the good you can, solely because God Himself will reward it. Like St. Paul, you should not be troubled

---

[46] 1 Cor. 4:5.

about the judgments of men, provided you have nothing to fear from the judgments of God.[47]

Ask our Lord, who is all-knowing and understanding, to help you to look for the good in others; to teach you to overlook, for the most part, the merely human element in others, for most sins are due to frailty, rather than to malice. Ask Christ to aid you in giving others at least a fair chance to defend themselves.

∞

God alone can judge a person

The best remedy for the habit of judging others is the practice of thinking of your own guilt and demerits before God when you are tempted to judge the guilt of somebody else. If you remember your own past secret sins, you will always be grateful that others do not know them, and you will be generous and kindly in any judgment you pass on others. St. Paul says, "Why do you pass judgment on your brother? Or . . . why do you despise your brother? For we shall all stand before the judgment seat of God."[48]

Only when all the love and the grace of God shall have been powerless to triumph in the unrighteous man and, for that reason, shall have been taken from him, then only will God judge that the time has come when He must cast him off with contempt. While an all-holy God waits and delays His judgment, our mind is soon made up and we say that we find it no longer possible to respect such a man. While God withholds His sentence, we have long ago condemned him.

St. James says, "There is one lawgiver and judge: He who is able to save and to destroy. But who are you that you judge your

[47] Cf. 1 Cor. 4:3-4.
[48] Rom. 14:10.

neighbor?"[49] Are you the right person to condemn anybody? Although you may not have some of the human weaknesses of your neighbor, you are not exempt from human frailty. The more deeply you look into yourself, the more clearly will you notice your own sinfulness. David prayed, "Behold, I was brought forth in iniquity, and in sin did my mother conceive me."[50] Once you have come to know yourself, you will lose all desire to sit in judgment upon others.

∞

Interpret the actions of others in the best light

Both justice and charity demand not only that you keep from judging the actions of others, but also that you interpret their actions in the best possible light. Nobody can judge people fairly except God, for He alone judges with perfect knowledge, certainty, and compassion. God is merciful because He is all-knowing and all-wise. In imitation of God, you must learn to interpret the motives and actions of others kindly before you can arrive at perfect love of your neighbor. Your kind interpretations are images of the merciful compassion of the Creator, who can find excuses for His creatures. Therefore, kindness in judging is true wisdom, because it is an imitation of the wisdom of God.

Have you not noticed in your past experience that your kind interpretations were almost always truer than your harsh ones? How many mistakes you have made in judging others! You have seen a thing as clear as day. It could have but one meaning. You have already formed an uncharitable judgment and roused your righteous indignation. All at once, the whole matter is differently

[49] James 4:12.
[50] Ps. 51:5.

and simply explained, so simply that you wonder why you had not thought of it yourself.[51]

It would be comparatively easy for you to be holy if only you could always see the characters of your neighbors in a favorable light. Of course, it would be unreal to grow blind to evil, but you must grow to something higher and truer than just a quickness in detecting evil.

The habit of kindness in judging others is very difficult to acquire. In fact, it is generally not acquired until very late in the spiritual life. In imitation of Jesus, the saints were most merciful; they sought in every possible way to protect the reputation of their fellowmen. You cannot do better than follow in their footsteps.

∞

Prejudice and bigotry are enemies of charity

When you persist in passing rash judgments, even though they are seldom accurate, and even stubbornly adhere to them, even though advised of their inaccuracy, you begin to cultivate a vice that is also a mental disease: prejudice. If you are prejudiced, you will never seek a reason for these aversions in yourself, but place the blame on another. When your prejudice extends to vast groups of men and you shut yourself off from them by a sort of spite-wall, you are suffering from a particularly harmful poison called bigotry.

Prejudice and bigotry find no room in the intelligent mind — a mind that is not only open to conviction, but also thirsting for justice and fair play. They are diseases that bring misguided judgments, aversions, and hatred. Hence prejudiced persons not only never speak well, but, in their narrowness, they can never think well of those whom they dislike, be they individuals or groups.

[51] Cf. Faber, *Spiritual Conferences*, 45.

Prejudice and bigotry are mists that, in your journey through the world, often dim and obscure the brightest and best of all the good and glorious objects that meet you on your way. They dwarf your soul by shutting out the truth.

If you are faced with such difficulties, remember the following considerations.

• *Do not allow pride to cloud your vision.* To feel superior to your neighbor because of your superior social standing or greater wealth or education is a foolish vice; tomorrow the tables may be reversed. And even if they are not, your neighbor, for all his defects, may be far more pleasing to God than you are.

• *Recall your own faults.* You probably have a fault to match every fault of the person you cannot get along with. So do not pass judgment.

• *Appreciate differences between people.* God had His good reasons for arranging matters so that people and families would be different. One of these reasons was so that all of us might have ample opportunity to practice the virtue of charity. It is easy to practice charity at a distance, but the real test comes in the close relationship of neighbor to neighbor. Even granting that your neighbor provokes you to uncharitableness, our Lord still insists, "Do good to those who hate you, and pray for those who persecute you."[52] Interpret literally and follow bravely our Lord's command: "Love your neighbor as yourself."[53]

[52] Cf. Luke 6:27; Matt. 5:44.
[53] Matt. 22:39.

- *Remember your duty as a genuine Christian.* Although your emotions and feelings may incline you to dislike or resent a particular national or racial group, strive to keep from being ruled by these emotions and feelings. Try to avoid in your speech slighting references to people of other nationalities, and, in acting, try to exercise genuine charity toward all.

Prejudice can be overcome by good will. We must remember that all men are children of God. If you really want to, you can do much to eliminate friction in your family and among your friends. What is more important, you will prove your right to the name Christian, since that means looking upon Christ as your brother and the brother of all human creatures, whatever their race or nationality.

Chapter Three

∞

Resist greed in all its forms

Love of gain and the practice of economy are part of the natural love of self that God Himself implanted in us. These natural virtues have been given to us in order that, by their means, we might make our own existence and well-being secure. There is nothing intrinsically wrong in a man's striving for wealth.

Greed pursues a similar aim, but with evil means. Greed, or covetousness, is an excessive desire for worldly possessions. It crushes all competitors, exploits workers, and acknowledges no other judge of its conduct than success. This is a serious obstacle to love of neighbor. Hence all thoughts and desires inspired by greed must be checked and banished from your soul.

Greed robs a person of love of neighbor. When one is dominated by greed, he soon comes to have no consideration or compassion, no generosity or love toward anyone. He looks upon others as so many obstacles in his way as he rushes on headlong to acquire greater wealth.

Greed robs a person of love of God. It is impossible to serve two masters, God and mammon.[54] Immoderate love of material goods

---

[54] Cf. Matt. 6:24.

entails the neglect of God. Greed even robs a person of all that he could really call his own and strips him of his only true wealth: the treasures of his soul. At death he will be stripped of all that greed has procured for him, because these goods are only borrowed.

Greed is the reason for much unhappiness. True contentment comes from finding happiness not in earthly things, but in God.

Jesus says, "Take heed, and beware of all covetousness; for a man's life does not consist in the abundance of his possessions."[55] He does not appeal so much to our love for others as to the right kind of love for ourselves. Thus, when He urged the rich young man to sell all his possessions and give the proceeds to the poor so that he might have an investment in Heaven,[56] He was thinking of the soul of the young man. St. John says, "Do not love the world or the things in the world. If anyone loves the world, love for the Father is not in him. For all that is in the world, the lust of the flesh, and the lust of the eyes, and the pride of life, is not of the Father, but is of the world. And the world passes away, and the lust of it; but he who does the will of God abides forever."[57]

If there is even a shred of greed in your heart, ask our Lord for the grace to overcome it and instead to fill your soul with an ardent desire for the things of God, which will enrich your soul and win for you an eternal reward.

∞

Envy is sadness over the good fortune of others

Envy, which is rooted in pride and vanity, is sadness over the good fortune of another because that good fortune stands in the

---

[55] Luke 12:15.

[56] Matt. 19:21.

[57] 1 John 2:15-17.

way of something that one desires for oneself. This undue appropriation to self of honor, esteem, position, power, and all that leads to it — money, talent, education, personality, or even the grace of God — may be incentives to envy. You are guilty of envy if you let your disappointment make you bitter and unkind, or induce you to scheme against those who have gotten ahead of you. The natural law and the tenth commandment — "Thou shalt not covet thy neighbor's goods" — stand against this tendency of human nature.

St. Paul says, "Love is not envious."[58] St. Augustine considers envy a monstrous vice. St. Thomas holds that it can be grievous, although, on account of trifling matter or lack of deliberation, it is usually only venial. But regret at another's success is not always wrong. The motive prompting it is the determining factor. It is excusable to be grieved because an influential person, openly hostile to the Church, is placed in a position of power, or if great wealth comes to a person who will abuse it.

Envy is the exact contrary of charity in thought, feeling, desire, and conduct. We are members of the Mystical Body of Christ and, in consequence, we must be mutual helps and supports to one another. Envy makes this impossible.

Love rejoices in good wherever it finds it; envy is pained by good, and the sight of the happiness of others hurts the eyes and the heart of the envious man. Love wishes to give; envy would rather receive. Love creates; envy destroys. Love builds up; envy pulls down. Love helps those in need, comforts the afflicted, and strives to turn all that is evil into good; envy would turn the little happiness to be found in this world into evil, sorrow, and pain.

Joy at another's misfortune, really revengefulness and spite, almost invariably accompanies envy. None of this is derived from

---

[58] Cf. 1 Cor. 13:4.

our Father in Heaven, who is infinite goodness and who can rejoice only in what is good. Delight in another's misfortune owes its origin to the Devil, who, in the depths of his own misery, knows no other pleasure than that which he finds in our pain.

∞

The evil effects of envy are very great

Envy disrupts social life generally. It sets the child against the father, brother against brother, neighbor against neighbor, and nation against nation. It kills friendship, undermines business relations, and hinders reconciliation. It is one of the chief sources of misunderstanding, criticism, hatred, vengeance, calumny, detraction, and perverse attacks on private life.

Envy and greed, the source of the world's unrest and wars, are sins against charity, because they make us seek what belongs to others. Often, even at the cost of harm to our neighbor, we want what does not belong to us.

But the most harmful consequences fall on the envious individual himself. Of all the passions, envy is the only one that yields nothing but pain. Envy has no reward for men. It gives no gratification, like lust or pride, but augments misery. Envy is like a gnawing worm that destroys peace of mind and health of body. It deteriorates character by filling the soul with despondency. The envious person becomes distrustful, unjust, and suspicious. Envy makes its victims ill-tempered, sad, and unapproachable.

The malice of envy is best recognized in the fall of the angels. They were cast out of Heaven because they envied God. The book of Wisdom says, "Through the Devil's envy, death entered the world."[59] Our first parents were the victims of Lucifer's envy.

[59] Wisd. 2:24.

Envy caused the first death in human history. Picture the terror of Abel when he beheld his brother, his face distorted by envy, about to deal him the murderous blow,[60] and the grief of mother Eve when her blood-stained child was laid at her feet. Or think of the gnawing anguish with which the dark envy of King Saul filled the life of youthful David.[61]

∞

Jealousy is a form of envy

Jealousy implies the fear of being displaced by a rival, or of being deprived of that which is rightfully ours or of that which we think ought to be ours.

Jealousy is another form of envy. Jealousy has to do with our own possessions, whereas envy has to do with the possessions of others. We resent an intrusion upon that which belongs to us, and we are prone to become revengeful on account of this disregard of our rights and claims.

Jealousy goes a step further than envy; it not only tries to lessen the good opinion others enjoy and criticizes those who are praised and rewarded, but is characterized by an excessive love of our own personal good and brings on a fear that we will be deprived of it. Jealousy prefers to see the good left undone rather than to lose a single degree of praise.

∞

Recognize the effects of jealousy

Jealousy is rooted in pride and, therefore, can become a hotbed where other vices grow. Hatred springs from jealousy, and the

---

[60] Cf. Gen. 4:8.
[61] Cf. 1 Sam. 18:8-9.

fruits of hatred are calumny, detraction, and rash judgment. Gossip is stimulated by jealousy and becomes the instrument by which characters and reputations can be harmed.

Jealousy can drive men to excess in work, ambition, and the quest for riches and even cause them to use questionable means to surpass their rivals. Thus loyalty and justice suffer. When jealousy is not satisfied, there is no peace of soul, but anguish and unhappiness.

Features of your character sometimes reveal themselves sharply during the playing of games, either of skill or of chance. To be able to lose a game with good grace and unaffected charity and humility is a sign of your willpower and dominance over pride and passion. If you are a poor loser, you will reveal your weakness of willpower by angry accusations against the winner, or by placing the blame for your failure on a partner or teammate or innocent bystander, or by showing great unhappiness and gloominess.

If you are a good loser, you recognize that games are intended for recreation and enjoyment, and that neither winning nor losing should be taken too seriously. Above all, you know that if the turn of fortune in a game robs you of peace or induces you to be unkind to others, then the game has defeated its purpose. You will also see that at times it is good for your humility for you to lose a game, and you should be thankful for the spiritual good that arises from a defeat.

∞

Jealousy is not always sinful

Jealousy is not necessarily an evil thing, but is quite lawful in defense of a claim to your rights if directed properly and kept within due limits. It may even be a duty. It is proper to be jealous of your rights and authority insofar as you possess them. You have a duty to defend your rights of worship, your rights as a citizen of a free country, and your rights to educate youth in principles of Catholicity. You must be jealous of these and similar rights.

Regarding your personal rights on the natural plane, the genuineness and beauty of charity are manifested by relinquishing those same rights not only ungrudgingly, but graciously and even gladly. It is to your best advantage to relinquish that which is your due for the sake of charity. Jesus said, "But I say to you, do not resist one who is evil. But if anyone strikes you on the right cheek, turn to him the other also; and if anyone would sue you and take your coat, let him have your cloak as well; and if anyone forces you to go one mile, go with him two miles. Give to him who begs from you, and do not refuse him who would borrow from you."[62]

St. Paul says, "Let each one not consider the things that are his own, but those that are other men's," and, "Let all men know your forbearance."[63] Forbearance indicates that virtue by which you are content not to demand all to which you have a claim in strict justice. St. Paul reminds us that Christ Himself has willingly relinquished His rights: "He . . . emptied Himself, taking the form of a servant, being born in the likeness of men."[64]

∞

Vainglory is an inordinate love of self

Vainglory is an expression of envy and jealousy and, therefore, an obstacle to brotherly love. Vainglory is an inordinate regard of self. It is self-conceit, the overestimation of one's powers — social position, learning or talent, or skill or ability. Self-love is so strong a tendency that you may be carried away by it to the extent of

---

[62] Matt. 5:39-42.

[63] Cf. Phil. 2:4 (Douay-Rheims edition); Phil. 4:5.

[64] Phil. 2:7.

embittering your life and, consequently, rendering yourself truly miserable.

St. Paul considers vainglory an obstacle to brotherly love. "Love is not arrogant or rude. Love does not insist on its own way."[65] Anyone who permits himself to be governed by vainglory easily arouses resentment in others. Anyone who fails to impress others by his own worthless pomp easily becomes a victim of envy himself.

Try to see how vainglory tends to belittle the good you do possess; how it tends to make you untrue, unhappy, and ridiculous in the eyes of others; how it spoils your character. You have received great favors and unmerited blessings from God. Of yourself, you are and have nothing, except sin. Left to yourself, you would be a slave to passion. Whatever is good in you is really due to the working of grace in your soul. Therefore, humility and gratitude should be natural to you.

Christ did not seek the esteem and praise of men. He sought only His Father's honor. By His way of life, He evoked the sharp criticism and bitter hatred of His own nation. Only true humility could stand that test of virtue. St. Paul says, "Christ did not please Himself, but, as it is written, 'The reproaches of those who reproached Thee fell upon me.' "[66]

Rather than pursue the esteem and recognition of men, seek the esteem of Christ through humble use of the talents He has given you. You will really want that esteem in the hour of your death. The psalmist says, "Not to us, O Lord, not to us, but to Thy name give glory."[67]

[65] Cf. 1 Cor. 13:5.
[66] Rom. 15:3.
[67] Ps. 115:1.

∞

Learn to resist greed, envy, and jealousy

Ask the Holy Spirit for the grace necessary to overcome the petty jealousies and expressions of vainglory that often mar the luster of your charity.

Sinful envy, jealousy, and vainglory are traceable to pride and greed, resulting from wounded self-love or undue self-esteem. These are passions that manifest themselves daily in human contacts. They exercise a great influence on human thoughts and desires. They modify feeling and control conduct. They are responsible for many sins of uncharitableness and many of the anxieties that rack the souls of men.

The sign of a true Christian is that he loves God and loves his neighbor as himself. Greed, envy, and jealousy breed hate, not love; hence, they have no place in the life of a follower of Christ. Therefore, St. Paul says, "Let us have no self-conceit, no provoking of one another, no envy of one another."[68]

The following suggestions may help you to avoid greed, envy, and jealousy:

• *Remember that your first purpose in life is to save your soul for Heaven.* Material things are to be used as means to that end, and are never to be permitted to stand in the way of attaining it. Christ said, "Seek first God's kingdom and His righteousness."[69]

Be solicitous for the increase of God's grace and peace in your soul. In the realm of God's grace, there is no cause for envy, because God's grace is limitless for all. It is almost entirely up to you in how far you possess God's grace.

[68] Gal. 5:26.
[69] Cf. Matt. 6:33.

• *Be humbly submissive to God's will.* He has imposed His laws of justice and charity on mankind so that all may work together to share adequately in the good things of earth. But in particular instances, He permits inequalities, injustices, and even persecution to befall some men, while He allows others, sometimes even the wicked, to prosper. This is by no means a sign of His favor. To avoid greed and envy, you must see in these things God's permissive will, which is ruled by His wisdom and His love.

Train yourself to be satisfied with what God has given you, and do not try to become what you are not. Control your ambitions and do not seek honors that are out of your reach. Do not strive for accomplishments that, perhaps, God does not want you to attain.

• *Never lose courage in the struggle against envy.* Very seldom can a heart be found that does not at times feel tempted to envy. A generous soul is humiliated to feel envy stirring within it, endeavoring to trouble its vision. So do not be surprised to detect envy trying to influence your thoughts, words, and deeds. You may be somewhat naturally inclined to rejoice at the failure of others and to be sad at their success. Let the temptation be an occasion for cultivating virtuous generosity and charity, as well as self-discipline. The more you have to combat temptations to envy, the deeper can the roots of charity be implanted in your life.

Build up a resistance against greed, envy, and jealousy by scorning them. Crush every jealous sentiment that shows itself. Distract your mind from every envious thought.

• *Imitate the good qualities you find in others*, rather than bewail them. Be sensible enough to see that the good qualities of others do not lessen your own. If your neighbor excels in one thing, he probably is mediocre in another in which you excel. Men differ from one another. God has given all of us varied talents and abilities. It is foolish to let envy and jealousy dim whatever brilliance God has given to each of us.

Imitating the good qualities of others will encourage you to work hard enough to surpass another in virtue, knowledge, and even holiness, and it will help you to seek recognition, not for yourself, but for God and the good of the Church and souls. A healthy emulation differs from jealousy, because its objective is right. It has worthy motives and is fair in all its means. The Church herself presents the saints to us as models of virtue so that we might imitate them. St. Paul urged the Corinthians to emulate him in his love for Christ: "Be imitators of me, as I am of Christ."[70]

• *Be kind to the person you envy.* Love alone can eradicate envy from your soul. Love is stronger than the envy that brought death into the world, stronger than the malicious joy that springs up when your neighbor is in trouble. St. Paul says, "Love does not rejoice at wrong."[71]

Always speak well of the person you envy. Praise his good qualities. Refuse to think and speak of the less complimentary things in his life. Defend him as prudence dictates, and excuse him as much as possible.

Rejoice in Christ when others are blessed with talents, gifts, success, and honors. We are all members of the Mystical Body of Christ. The good qualities of one part of the Body redound to the well-being of all the other parts. Pray

[70] 1 Cor. 11:1.
[71] Cf. 1 Cor. 13:6.

much for the success of your neighbor's undertakings, and thank God for the good he does. Let charity breathe a short prayer that God may preserve the good fortune of your neighbor and ward off from him all harm. Such a prayer breaks the power of envy and banishes evil joy from your heart.

• *Remain close to God* through continued prayer and the frequent reception of the sacraments of Penance and Holy Communion. This is the normal way to receive grace. Only when your soul is aided by God's grace will right convictions about these things flourish in your heart. If you do not remain close to God, you will find yourself gradually becoming more and more attached to the things of the world, and that means that you will become more and more a victim of the vices of greed and envy.

Envy, once it has taken hold of man, is very difficult to uproot. The reason for this is the blindness of the soul, a result of envy, and the persistent unwillingness to admit even to oneself the guilt of a vice so thoroughly denounced by everyone. Envy is a vice difficult to overcome, but nothing is impossible with the grace of God. Put all your confidence in God, and repel promptly all temptations to envy, greed, and jealousy. Ask for the grace always to wish others well in their works.

Chapter Four

∞

Control inordinate anger

Anger is an inordinate feeling of displeasure at a real or supposed injury, with a desire to punish the offender. Your anger is inordinate when the correction or punishment that you administer is motivated by passion and fury. For instance, you may use bitter words against another person, not in order to correct or help, but only to hurt that person for the sake of taking revenge; or you may become peevish and bear grudges in an effort to get back at somebody.

Your anger is inordinate when the methods that you use are wrong — such as cursing, profanity, screaming, or cruelty. These are sinful in themselves and are capable of doing more harm than good.

Although you seldom permit yourself to give way to anger toward strangers, acquaintances, and friends, you may often permit anger to show itself in your family, which is the most sacred relationship in life. Parents sin when they use profanity in correcting their children, when they inflict punishment far beyond reasonable limits, and when they shout at their children at the top of their voices and thereby attempt to frighten them. You carry out your duty of correcting others reasonably only when reason, not passion, inspires it, and the words and actions you use are designed to help and not hurt the one you correct.

Your anger is inordinate when you administer correction or punishment when you are in no position to do so. Anger is sometimes used as a form of defense; for example, a person who has been guilty of serious faults blasts out against others in an attempt to distract attention from his own faults.

Anger is an enemy of charity. Anger is a violent disturbance of the feelings and, by its very nature, destructive. You are hardly ever more unjust toward your neighbor than when you are angry, because you do not stop to think whether that which you strike is in any way at fault or not.

Anger is an injustice — often an unconscious injustice against God Himself, who is infinite goodness. Thus every lack of charity of an angry man is also a lack of love toward God, for any injury done to your neighbor is accounted as done to God Himself.

Every kind of injustice merits God's punishment. Punishment may be said to begin with the first moment of anger. The distorted features proclaim that the angered man is in pain. Not only does anger make you ridiculous in your looks, words, and actions, but it also causes harm. It harms your health; it makes you miserable and unhappy; it obscures your thinking and renders you unable to judge correctly.

By anger you may destroy the peace of a serene day or hurt your dearest one. By your anger you may break up a noble and long-standing friendship. Anger may force you to utter insults for which you have to apologize. It can embarrass you and spoil many material advantages and even dishonor your character. Many people have had to lament during a lifetime the mischief done in a moment of anger. But who can imagine the bitter regrets during all eternity?

∞

Anger may be mortally or venially sinful

Anger is *mortally* sinful if your feelings of displeasure turn into passion and get beyond the control of reason. The mortal sin of anger consists of the deliberate desire or the attempt to hurt somebody seriously or to see somebody hurt seriously. Jesus said, "Everyone who is angry with his brother shall be liable to judgment."[72]

Anger is *venially* sinful if it is caused by a merely accidental injury, if you are more displeased with the offender than with the offense, or if it tempts you to inflict excessive punishment. Most people do not desire to hurt seriously the one who provoked their anger. They desire to hurt that person only enough to satisfy their own pride and selfishness.

With most of us, it is the small and petty manifestations of anger that are in need of curbing and control. You probably have the tendency to express impatience over the small faults of those around you.

Irritability is the flaw of character whereby you allow yourself to be unpleasant, curt, and ill-mannered with others for no other reason than that you do not happen to be feeling just right. It shows itself when nothing has been said or done that could possibly be construed as an offense.

If you are irritable, you make many false excuses for your weakness. You will say that your irritability is caused by your nerves, high or low blood pressure, insomnia, indigestion, or worries and responsibilities. All such excuses are usually a false front. Irritability is a lack of self-control, an inability to subject your feelings to the demands of charity. Irritability is immaturity of character. If you are subject to being cross and unpleasant with others for no

[72] Matt. 5:22.

apparent reason, you need to come face-to-face with the fact that you are thinking too much of yourself. After all, your feelings are not the most important thing in this world.

Therefore, most of the forms in which you manifest anger toward another are venial sins. This fact should not lessen your desire to overcome them. Such venial sins can, if they go unchecked, lead to mortal sins, and that can completely destroy the happiness of a home and the peace that should prevail among men.

☙

Sometimes anger is not sinful

There is a legitimate anger. A legitimate anger is itself a likeness of the anger of divine justice. If you are angry only when you are in the presence of an evident and grievous fault of another and if, acting as the instrument of divine wrath, you strictly apportion the punishment to the offense, your anger may be a just indignation. St. James says, "Let every man be quick to hear, slow to speak, slow to anger, for the anger of man does not work the righteousness of God."[73] Thus the apostle warns us against anger, but he does not say we should never be angry at all; rather, he says that we should be "slow to anger."

Anger can at times be justified. Our Lord wasted no time in getting a whip and driving from the Temple the sellers who had turned the house of God into a marketplace.[74] If a mother, then, not just for the sake of getting the poison of anger out of her system, but out of a responsibility tempered with love, shows anger and backs up that anger with chastisement of a child, she has gained, not lost, favor with God.

[73] James 1:19-20.
[74] Cf. John 2:14-16.

But remember how easy it is to exaggerate your neighbor's guilt, especially when, by his conduct, he has injured not so much God's interests as your own. In such circumstances, your anger may lead to a sin against justice and charity.

It will ease your conscience to remember that there is a distinction between *feelings* of anger and *sins* of anger. At some time or another, you will *feel* angry or impatient with others, or be tempted to a bitter answer, or be carried away by an interior resentment against somebody else. Such feelings are in no sense sinful if you keep them from appearing in your external conduct in any way, and if you do not permit them to lead to deliberate desires that others be hurt in some way. You can control these feelings only by self-discipline and God's grace.

There is a distinction between the sin of anger and reasonable, forceful attempts to correct others who are subject to your authority and influence and who are in need of correction. Therefore, anger is not sinful if you are displeased but do not desire to hurt; if, although you dislike the fault, you are trying to control your anger; or if you seek to punish the hurt in a reasonable way. Nevertheless, such anger rises from pride, envy, and jealousy.

∞

Overcome your anger through meekness

Anger is overcome by meekness. Our Lord said, "Blessed are the meek, for they shall inherit the earth."[75] Meekness is not weakness. Far from weakness, it takes the very strength of God to be meek.

In his *Introduction to the Devout Life*, St. Francis de Sales tells us, "The person who possesses Christian meekness is affectionate

[75] Matt. 5:5.

and tender toward everyone; he is disposed to forgive and excuse the frailties of others; the goodness of his heart appears in a sweet affability that influences his words and actions, presents every object to his view in the most charitable and pleasing light. He never admits in his speech any harsh expression, much less any term that is haughty or rude. An amiable serenity is always painted in his countenance, which distinguishes him remarkably from those violent characters who, with looks full of fury, know only how to refuse, or who, when they grant, do it with so bad a grace that they lose all the merit of the favor they bestow.

St. Francis de Sales left us the following practical advice as a remedy against anger: "A most important means for acquiring the habit of interior mildness is to accustom ourselves to perform all our actions and to speak all our words, whether important or not, quietly and gently. Multiply these acts as much as you can in tranquillity; so you will accustom your heart to gentleness."

Never allow yourself to fall into a passion, nor open the door to anger on any pretext whatsoever. For once it has gained an entrance, it is no longer in your power to banish it or moderate it.

The remedies against anger are three:

* *Diversion:* check anger immediately by diverting your mind to some other object, and do not speak a word.

* *Prayer:* imitate the apostles when they beheld the tempest at sea,[76] and have recourse to God, for it belongs to Him alone to restore peace to your soul.

* *Counterattacks:* should you feel that anger has already gained a foothold in your heart, do whatever you can to

[76] Cf. Matt. 8:24-25.

regain your composure. Then endeavor to make acts of humility and kindness toward the person against whom you are irritated. This, however, must be done with mildness, for it is of the utmost importance not to reopen the wounds.

If you are one in whom Original Sin breaks out in the angry fester of temper, try to understand that there is more thoughtlessness than malice in the world. People are not out to offend you deliberately and maliciously. But all of us are thoughtless at times and do not readily realize that our words and actions are going to hurt people. That is why many people do not even know what you are raving about. You may have seen old friends break apart over some little matter that meekness would have easily settled.

The pride of life, which St. John set down as one of the three root causes of evil in the world, manifests itself at times in your life in the form of impatience and anger with those around you. This is one fault in your character that you probably most easily excuse and even defend.

Do not excuse or defend outbursts of anger in an offhand manner by saying, "If people make me angry, I won't be responsible for what I say or do." This means you will be twice as responsible, because you know beforehand where and how temptation will strike. You may make the excuse: "I get angry often, but I just can't help it." What you really mean is that you love your fault so much that you refuse to make the effort required to rid yourself of it, or else you are just too lazy to make the effort to overcome the habit.

If you want a strong character, never compromise with any fault. Admit it humbly and, with every admission, make a renewed determination to overcome it with the help of God. The faults that produce bad characters are often the faults that are loved and defended.

The passion of anger is most difficult to bring under perfect control. If you are predisposed to it by temperament, you will have to spend a lifetime fighting against the tendency to become violently angry when you are crossed. Do not concede to discouragement at repeated setbacks.

You must make tireless efforts to reach the ideal of self-mastery. This self-mastery means silence in moments of provocation and postponement of action when you are emotionally upset. God's grace is able to do what you cannot do because of your weakness. That grace is secured through the sacraments and prayer. At Confession and after Holy Communion, ask Jesus to help you to control your temper. When you are tempted to be angry, repeat the invocation: "Jesus, meek and humble of heart, make my heart like unto Thine." If you have been unsuccessful in controlling your temper, be sorry for your fault at once and say, "My Jesus, mercy!" The grace of God will enable you to be meek and gentle, like the Master, and, following His example, you will inherit the land. Every victory helps to harness the strong forces of passion and emotion within you. If these forces are disciplined, they are capable of accomplishing great things.

Why not pick out one person or situation that can make you get angry suddenly? Work on that alone. Plan ahead how you are going to handle that person or situation. No matter what happens, do not let yourself get out of control around that one person or in that one situation. If you fail, confess the fault sincerely. You will gradually find a sense of control spreading throughout your day, within your family life, and among your associates.

Our Lord encouraged you to learn meekness from Him because He is meek and humble of heart.[77] Learn of Him, not because of

[77] Matt. 11:29.

the perfect example He gave you for fortitude and temperance and other virtues, but because He is meek.

St. Margaret Mary[78] explains the effects of meekness: "The virtue of meekness will make you condescending toward your neighbor whom you will excuse, bearing charitably and in silence all the pain which may be caused. . . . If you wish to become a disciple of the Sacred Heart of Jesus, you must conform yourself to His divine maxims and be meek and humble like Him."

You know what Jesus meant when He said that you have to be *in* the world and not *of* it, and that, if you wanted to follow Him, you could expect disappointments and even insults. The disciple is not above the Master, and the world crucified the Master. Even if you cannot understand the reason for meekness, try to become meek because Christ was meek. Learn of Him, for meekness is the price of peace in your heart and family, peace in your little corner of the world.

When you must suffer, think of the Master standing head and shoulders above those who were taunting Him. All the strength of God was shining through His eyes as He stood there and took all they had to give, even as He would hang there and ask forgiveness for them, and at the end, win back a thief[79] and gain an eternal kingdom.

---

[78] St. Margaret Mary Alacoque (1647-1690), Visitation nun and chief founder of devotion to the Sacred Heart of Jesus.

[79] Cf. Luke 23:39-42.

Chapter Five

Learn to bear others' offenses with kindness

An aversion is an unexplainable feeling of dislike or distaste for a certain person. It is not based on any real injury, nor can it be explained by the usual things that may cause dislike, such as jealousy, envy, rivalry, or ambition. An aversion is sometimes based upon some kind of misunderstanding. It may be the result of conflicting temperaments and characters so that you are almost instinctively annoyed by the way another person speaks and acts. Moreover, a person may arouse aversion and at the same time be admired by others.

Aversion may seem to be a small subtle energy of the human heart, yet its strength is sometimes able to overwhelm true charity. When a person of a naturally kind disposition cannot bring himself to speak a kind word to some particular person near him, although the person may be harmless, the force of aversion acts like an evil spell. This power that takes speech from your mouth and warmth from your heart comes from some defect in your own self.

It is not a sin to experience such emotions. But it is sinful to give way to them and to allow yourself to be swept off your feet without resistance. God wills that you should make a real effort to restore at least some of your former peace of soul. This can be achieved only by diverting or checking these feelings as soon as you feel them welling up in your soul, but especially by filling your heart with a spirit of charity.

You show aversion by letting people know how you feel about the person you do not like and by adding some bitter comment about the person's faults, real or imaginary.

You show aversion by your impolite and uncharitable conduct toward the person you dislike by answering questions sharply and ridiculing or even insulting the person with what appear to be humorous remarks. Sometimes you will defend yourself in all this by saying that to act otherwise would be hypocrisy, although it is never hypocrisy to hide one's baser emotions.

You show aversion also by refusing to take part in any work or recreation if the person you dislike is involved. It is grossly uncharitable to prefer to see a good work undone, or a good time spoiled, rather than cooperate with a person you dislike.

∞

Learn to overcome aversions

You can overcome feelings of aversion by diverting or checking them as soon as you realize that they are welling up in your soul; by hiding them from others and being silent about them; by manifesting special kindness toward the person you dislike whenever this is possible; by remembering that you may be a source of aversion to others; by being convinced that you cannot love God if you do not love even your enemies; and by making a regular practice of praying for those you dislike.

You may never acquire a mastery of your feelings, nor is it really necessary. It will be best — once you have rid yourself of every conscious external manifestation of aversion — to aim not so much at covering up your feelings of dislike, but rather to strive for a complete mastery of them. The big test of true charity in your life is your attitude and habitual conduct toward those whose personalities awaken in you a reaction of aversion.

St. James says, "Draw near to God, and He will draw near to you. Cleanse your hands, you sinners, and purify your hearts, you men of double mind."[80] Having cleansed your heart by the clear stream of charity, you will turn every aversion, slowly and silently, to real attraction and genuine charity.

∞

Be vigilant against becoming resentful

Resentment is closely allied to aversion as a foe of charity. The resentful person does not want to hurt and wound others as does the angry or revengeful person. Proudly and silently, resentment shuts itself in and gives itself up to the bitterness and gloom of its reactions and memories. It tries not to betray itself outwardly by a gracious word or a kind deed. When love is thus shut up in the heart, it is bound to wither and die.

You may be in most things a generous person, yet resentment can get a footing in your heart. If you have been misunderstood, or feel deeply hurt by the ingratitude and injustice of another, do not withdraw into solitude and there brood over your painful memories. Take the advice of St. Paul: "Do not let the sun go down on your anger, and give no opportunity to the Devil."[81] If your feelings have been hurt, do not tear open your wounds. Stop dwelling on the cruel word that has been spoken to you; forget the mean way in which someone has behaved toward you. Nothing does so much

[80] James 4:8.
[81] Eph. 4:26-27.

good to the soul as a love that pardons all things. The thought that God loves you should fill your heart with peace and joy.

How gladly you would forgive others were you to know that tomorrow would bring the death of the person you resent. Tomorrow might bring your own death. How painful to have to appear before God with this resentment in your soul! Yet you expect that God will meet you without anger and forget the wounds you inflicted on His heart by your sins.

At the close of day, when its bitter experiences stand out before you, be determined to forget all. You can go to sleep in peace with such sentiments in your heart.

∞

Harbor no grudges

To bear a grudge means to manifest prolonged resentment against someone for some real or doubtful or imagined offense that has been offered. This is expressed by a cold silence, by a refusal to take part in conversation or answer questions, by an aloofness from the one who has awakened the grudge, by sarcasm, biting comments, and caustic interpretations of another's conduct and words, and by sadness.

This angry silence charges the atmosphere with tension that can be sensed as easily as violent words. Sensitive and moody persons find themselves especially tempted to show their anger in this way. When they are angry at someone, they make him feel it by showing absolutely no interest in anything, not even in things that are ordinarily their favorite topics or activities. If accused of pouting, they adopt an attitude of sadness and answer every attempt to shake them out of it with a remark such as: "Just leave me alone."

The grudge-bearing person usually considers himself so right that he is perfectly justified in his conduct. He should see himself as others see him — as just a childish, pouting, self-opinionated weakling.

If you are guilty of the fault of bearing a grudge, you will overcome it only when you learn to make allowances both for the shortcomings of others and for your own touchy sensitiveness. Strength of character means the ability to overcome resentment against others, to hide hurt feelings, and to forgive quickly. There is little hope that you will overcome your bad habit unless you face the fact that your temperament inclines you to take offense where none is intended and then to lapse into an angry silence.

When somebody hurts or angers you, do not show your anger by withdrawing into a shell and refusing to talk. You may learn later that the one who provoked your anger was completely unaware of what it was that upset you. Do not be sensitive and touchy in your dealings with others, quick to perceive slights and slurs and slow to forget them. Do not show by your bearing and by the expression of your face or by a cool silence that you were slighted or hurt.

Do not express exaggerated humility when others disagree with you or insist on making them apologize frequently. Avoid dreaming about bitter answers to people who have humiliated you.

St. Margaret Mary gives us this advice: "Never keep up any coldness toward your neighbor, or else the Sacred Heart of Jesus Christ will keep aloof from you. When you resentfully call to mind former slights that you have received, you oblige our Lord to recall your past sins which His mercy had made Him forget." And again: "Bear patiently the little vexations caused by your neighbor's being of a disposition contrary to your own; do not show your resentment, for that displeases the Sacred Heart of our Lord."

If you have the tendency deliberately to nurse past grievances, remember the warning of Christ, that if you are not willing to forgive your enemies, you have no right to expect forgiveness from God for your own sins.[82] In business, in marriage, in any human field, try to develop a forgetful spirit insofar as past injuries are concerned. This will enable you to be more charitable in your judgments about others.

∞

Resist revengefulness

Revengefulness, born of aversion and resentment, is also an enemy of charity. Anger may express itself in attempts to take revenge on the one who occasioned it.

Some people have a strange tendency never to forget an injury, whether imaginary or real. They can even rejoice in situations that give them an opportunity to retaliate in some way. Much unpleasantness in human relationships arises from such a habit.

There is hardly a greater sign of weakness of character in a human being than the habit of trying to get even with others for every real or imaginary wrong that is committed. The weak character has a passion for revenge. He cannot leave judgment and punishment to God, but is constantly scheming to make someone suffer for hurting him.

Revenge may adopt a threefold course. First, revenge seeks to harm a person's good name by lessening the esteem that others have for him and causing him to be disliked. This can easily be detected by the bitter language used, the intensity of feeling, and the petty charges. Second, revenge tries to spoil a good work being done by another. A revengeful person is made peculiarly happy by the failures of his enemy and is even happier if he can contribute to those failures. Thus he will sow discord among the companions

[82] Cf. Matt. 6:15.

and associates of the one on whom he is taking revenge and will urge no cooperation. Finally, revenge tries to prevent the advancement of another. It stoops to the most vicious kind of lying.

Refuse to be moved to act out of revenge. You cannot go through life without being hurt and mistreated by others at some time or other. Take such things in stride, and refuse absolutely to be moved to words or actions against these others by mere revenge. Always discount largely anything said in a spirit of revenge, because it may be a total lie. If someone angers you, do not seek revenge by running that person down in your conversation with others, revealing his secret faults, and perhaps even exaggerating them and lying about them. Never try to alienate the friends of someone with whom you are angry, by making that person appear to be unworthy of their friendship or trust, or by spoiling that person's chances for advancement.

If you seek to take revenge against another, you have an exaggerated or wrong sense of justice, and little regard for Christian charity. Our Lord insisted not only that His followers are not to strike back at those who injure them, but that when they are struck on one cheek, they should turn the other for another blow.[83] This was His way of saying that revenge is sinful and will be punished by Him in the end.

∞

Do not let hatred take root in you

Hatred is persevering bad will. It is the deliberate crystallizing of one's anger into a state of enmity. It is worse than anger, aversion, resentment, and revengefulness. These injure charity, and quench it by degrees, but hatred puts it out at one blow.

[83] Matt. 5:39.

Where God is, there is light. Jesus said, "I am the light of the world; he who follows me will not walk in darkness, but will have the light of life."[84] Hatred is the opposite of charity; hence, it is also the opposite of the kingdom of God and of the kingdom of light. The spirit of hatred is the spirit of darkness. A man who hates is a blind man. He may take many steps that bring others nearer to God — he may go to church and pray — but he gets no nearer to the light so long as there is hatred in his heart. He walks in the darkness of separation from God.

St. John says, "He who loves his brother abides in the light, and in it there is no cause for stumbling. But he who hates his brother is in the darkness and walks in the darkness, and does not know where he is going, because the darkness has blinded his eyes."[85] The beloved disciple stated the sober, unvarnished truth when he declared, "Anyone who hates his brother is a murderer, and you know that no murderer has eternal life abiding in him."[86]

Hatred is sinful when it is a deliberate act of the will. It is hatred when you allow yourself to settle down to an abiding ill will toward a person who in some way blocks your desires and checks your progress, or treats you with scorn. This results in wishing him every evil or even deliberately returning evil for evil.

However, do not be troubled if you feel a strong sensory antipathy. This is not necessarily deliberate hatred and is no sin at all if you can successfully conceal it. You may say to yourself of another, "I can't bear to look at him." Such words are simple statements of fact and no sin if you have never resolved to do evil to that person and especially if you pray that God may bless and prosper him.

[84] John 8:12.
[85] 1 John 2:10-11.
[86] 1 John 3:15.

If hate has crept into your heart, you must battle with this evil spirit more obstinately than with an enemy who would rob you of your eyesight. Even though the angel of darkness may have the strength of a giant, he is powerless against a child of the light. Fortunately, love alone is all-powerful.

Try to counteract every desire to hurt another. Do not rejoice in the grave misfortune of an enemy, or refuse to pray for him, or refuse even to greet him when you meet alone or in the presence of others.

Deliberately to hate a fellow human being is the equivalent of hating God. This is inviting God's condemnation on yourself. Only in the measure in which you are willing to forgive those who have wronged you can you expect God to forgive you. And it does not matter how great is the wrong you have received from another person.

∽

Malice, meanness, and violence are forms of hate

Malice is the worst kind of hate. Hate often keeps within the sphere of our thoughts and feelings, whereas malice impels to action. Malice may have grown out of some bitter experience or some disappointment — a bitter word, an argument, a sneer.

Meanness is the habit of taking pleasure in small hurts inflicted on others. One of the marks of malice, it is aware of its inability to achieve anything great; hence, it tries to destroy human happiness, at least in little things.

Any hurt inflicted on a neighbor that is not obviously and objectively directed to his spiritual or material welfare is the fruit of meanness. Some people are mean without realizing it; others hurt their neighbor but justify the meanness on some righteous grounds. Meanness is the younger brother of cruelty.

You are guilty of meanness when you tell a person how much he is disliked by a third person, or what unkind things have been said about him in his absence; when you criticize some cherished possession of another, or some accomplished work of which he can be proud; when you call a person by a name that is highly offensive to him; when you ridicule the natural defects or bodily deformities of another, or his nationality, race, or religion; when you laugh in the face of a person who makes mistakes in grammar or speech; when you frighten people by wild tales of imminent danger; and when you draw attention repeatedly to a person's mistakes, even after they have been atoned for and corrected. The hurt inflicted by such deeds of uncharitableness will vary according to the sensitiveness and refinement of the person involved.

Violence is the tendency of unrestrained anger to hurt, by words and even by actions, the person who has aroused anger. It is one of the worst forms that anger or malice can take.

Violence is shown, for instance, when a parent strikes a child in a fury of passion that reveals a willingness to hurt him severely, or uses cruel instruments of punishment, or breaks things in giving way to anger. Violence may constitute a mortal sin if serious injury is attempted or done to another.

If you permit anger to lead to unreasonable violence, you reveal yourself to be immature and spoiled. If you really want to reform, you must do so by adopting a program of self-denial that will discipline your childish nature.

Malice is not only a human weakness, but is also the work of a power hostile to God. We are reminded of "the evil one"[87] of whom Holy Scripture speaks, whose aim is to pervert and to distort God's creation. A person remains in the power of this spirit as

[87] Matt. 13:19.

long as he yields to malice, and, in this condition, he is apart from God. God is goodness itself. He is without malice. St. John says, "God is love, and he who abides in love abides in God, and God abides in him."[88]

Every one of us has a place assigned to him at the banquet of life. We should ever remember the advice of St. Paul: "Let us, therefore, celebrate the festival, not with the old leaven, the leaven of malice and evil, but with the unleavened bread of sincerity and truth."[89]

---

[88] 1 John 4:16.
[89] 1 Cor. 5:8.

∞

Chapter Six

Recognize the consequences of unkind thoughts

To recognize clearly the serious consequences of uncharitable judgments in daily life will serve as a deterrent to the evil practice of judging others unkindly.

∞

Unkind judgments may be visited upon you

Uncharitableness in judging others torments the soul. Even a well-founded suspicion more or less degrades you. Although your suspicion may be verified, and you may escape from some material harm, you are the worse for having entertained it.

While virtue grows in your soul under the influence of kindly judgments, your unkind judgments concerning others are often visited upon you. You may fall into the sin of which you have judged another guilty. Or you may suddenly be overwhelmed with unusual temptations that remind you that the sin to which you are unexpectedly tempted is one you have been attributing to others.

Sometimes you yourself, although innocent, are falsely accused and believed to be guilty of a fault. Maybe the fault is one of which you have recently, in your own mind at least, accused another.

Once you have acquired the habit of judging others unfavorably, you will find it very easy to pass from judging trivial matters to those involving serious sin. Common sense tells you that a person himself is very much what he thinks of others. When you hear a person attribute meanness to another, you may be almost sure not only that the critic is an ill-tempered person, but that he has a similar element of meanness in himself, or is fast acquiring it.

∞

Unkind thoughts incur God's punishment

The most disastrous consequence of uncharitable thoughts is incurring the guilt of sin and the punishment of God. Uncharitable thoughts can be mortal or venial according to attendant circumstances. In the letter to the Romans, St. Paul speaks of serious sin and its inevitable consequence — eternal punishment: "You have no excuse, O man, whoever you are, when you judge another; for in passing judgment upon him, you condemn yourself, because you, the judge, are doing the very same things. We know that the judgment of God rightly falls upon those who do such things. Do you suppose, O man, that when you judge those who do such things and yet do them yourself, you will escape the judgment of God? Or do you presume upon the riches of His kindness and forbearance and patience? Do you not know that God's kindness is meant to lead you to repentance?

"But by your hard and impenitent heart, you are storing up wrath for yourself on the day of wrath, when God's righteous judgment will be revealed. For He will render to every man according to his works: to those who, by patience in well-doing, seek glory and honor and immortality, He will give eternal life; but for those who are factious and do not obey the truth, but obey wickedness, there will be wrath and fury. There will be tribulation and distress

94

for every human being who does evil, the Jew first and also the Greek, but glory and honor and peace for everyone who does good, the Jew first and also the Greek. For God shows no partiality."[90]

God evaluates the real merits of each individual with impartial justice. He is not controlled by considerations outside the case, such as the position, honor, talent, beauty, or wealth of the person concerned. God judges "rightly." On the Last Day, He will grant everlasting life to those who persevered in good works. But He will measure out "wrath and fury" to those who "obey wickedness." This means eternal punishment, with its torture for the body and its affliction and anguish for the soul.

Our Lord's warning is clear: "Judge not, that you be not judged. For with the judgment you pronounce you will be judged, and the measure you give will be the measure you get."[91]

Do not misconstrue God's patience toward you in the past. The kindness of God, manifested in His blessings freely given to you, together with His patience, is His way of urging you to repentance. In the spirit of humble gratitude for God's infinite patience with you, refrain from judging others.

It is very foolish to delude yourself into thinking that God will be partial to you and not punish you too severely for your sins. Refrain from such smug self-security. If St. Paul thought it worthwhile reminding the Roman converts of the serious truth of Hell in order to make their love for Christ more stable and generous, it is worth your while to think about it to urge you to prove your love for Christ by keeping His great commandment of love.

[90] Rom. 2:1-11.
[91] Matt. 7:1-2.

Chapter Seven

∞

Found your thoughts on virtue

A person's interior and exterior life arises and takes shape from his silent world of thought. Your earthly fortune may be built, and your eternal destiny will be decided, from the way you think. Your silent thoughts are like the roots of a plant. They remain hidden in the dark recesses of the earth, but from them stems the whole plant — its life and form, its strength and beauty. From them and through them the plant lives and dies. So, too, your thoughts, although hidden, are your real, vital force.

If you want to be pleasing to God and to grow in holiness, you must strive to develop kind thinking. If you have a correct world of thought, your soul will be healthy and your whole approach to life will be correct. And in no field of spiritual endeavor will your efforts be so necessary and so rewarding as in love of neighbor.

The opportunities for the practice of kind thoughts are countless. But such a practice takes generous and continuous effort.

∞

Avoid being suspicious

Mutual trust is one of the noblest expressions of charity. Love's first quality is mutual understanding, and its highest quality is faith in one another, because charity refuses to think evil. St. Paul says, "Love is patient and kind. . . . It does not rejoice at wrong. . . . Love bears all things, believes all things, hopes all things, endures all things."[92]

Suspicion, on the other hand, is an opinion, not too well-grounded, or grounded in false assumptions, that another has an evil purpose in a certain line of conduct. A suspicious person somehow adopts the general assumption that everybody must be deemed guilty of evil until he has proved himself to be innocent. Worst of all, he must always give expression to his suspicions in the hope of making others share them with him.

Many spoil all the relationships of private life by foolish suspicions, such as the husband who is constantly indulging suspicions about his wife, and vice versa; the parent who, without sufficient reason, is suspicious of his children; and the person who suspects his friends of talking about him behind his back or of pursuing, through friendship, some personal interest.

An unjustifiable lack of trust hurts deeply. If you set a low value on the moral worth of another, misjudge his dispositions, drag down his character, misinterpret his intentions, or torture his innocence by false suspicions and accusations, you inflict upon him one of life's bitterest trials. A trial like this caused the heart of the Lamb of God to be wrung with anguish in the Garden of Gethsemane. The whole story of Good Friday is summed up in false suspicions.

Mistrust leads astray. Not only unjustifiable mistrust, but at times even well-founded mistrust is a force that drags one down into the depths. When a man is aware that he is being suspected of a sin, he sometimes experiences a desire to commit that very sin and so to take yet another step on the downward path.

[92] 1 Cor. 13:4, 6-7.

The habit of being suspicious is not only destructive of all friendship and of the joys of social life; it also makes peace of heart almost impossible. St. Benedict[93] says that a suspicious man knows no rest. Suspicion robs us of interior peace as well as of external tranquillity. No one loves a suspicious man; he is involved in endless strife and wins no one's confidence. This trait makes some people very unpleasant companions and even very unpleasant acquaintances.

∞

Trust engenders happiness

True charity is incapable of thinking evil, not only because it is itself free from evil, but also because it has no love for anything that is evil. If you yourself are pure and kind and free from all deceit, you will readily see in everybody else a pure, good, and kindly person.

Trust is a better philosophy of life than suspicion. Suspicion is like an overzealous watchman who not only frightens off thieves, but likewise robs his master of all rest. This is true even if charity is often deceived and cheated and suffers many a loss that could have been prevented by a little suspicion.

Suspicion brings on unhappiness, whereas confidence and trust encourage content. Even when your confidence has been betrayed, in spite of the pain of disappointment, you feel happier than if you had to acknowledge that you have unjustly suspected another. Show confidence, and you will reap peace and happiness.

When it is wholly justified, trust urges us to do what is right, to take a step upward to make ourselves worthy of the confidence

---

[93] Possibly St. Benedict (c. 480-c. 550), father of Western monasticism. — ED.

that has been placed in us. Trust is one of the great educating and healing forces of life. When others give us their confidence, we are refreshed and cheered. If we wish to make men better, we must think better of them.

But trust does not mean that you must go through life giving your confidence to everyone whom you meet. When you have serious misgivings and positive facts, your love will not cease to hope and pray for the best and to cherish faith in the person's honesty. You will, however, be cautious in giving your confidence. But whenever the balance of good and bad opinion keeps fluctuating, your love will take the side of good opinion.

If you are inclined to be suspicious, the only cure is to acquire the habit of suppressing ungrounded rumors that come to your mind. Follow the practice of accepting people as good unless they objectively prove themselves to be bad. Learn to forgive those individuals who are guilty of evil conduct in any form.

Believe in others. Learn to forgive those who are guilty of evil conduct of any kind. High esteem is due to all human beings, since Christ loved all so deeply that He died for their salvation. His perfect charity is expressed in His prayer: "Father, forgive them."[94]

∞

Try to be agreeable

Charity requires unity of thought. St. Paul exhorts the Philippians to be one in mind, that is, to think alike and to love the same things, with one soul and one mind. He says, "Complete my joy by being of the same mind, having the same love, being in full accord and of one mind."[95]

[94] Luke 23:34.
[95] Phil. 2:2.

Forgetting the chains that bound him in his prison cell, St. Paul was concerned with the thought of repressing the dissensions that disturbed the Christian community. He reminded the Christians that, since there were so many ties that united them, they had to put aside what divided them. After twenty centuries of Christianity, this urgent appeal is not less pertinent today.

"One heart and soul"[96] was the slogan of the first followers of Christ. Unity merited for them the recognition by the pagans of their outstanding brotherly love. In accordance with this exhortation, you may look into your own unity of thought with your fellowmen, at least in all things lawful. You are contentious if you are given to quarrelsomeness, to bickering, and to finding fault habitually with others.

Never be a disturber of the peace by selfish tendencies and a quarrelsome disposition. Try to make an effort to cultivate approbation for things agreeable to the majority in the groups of persons with whom you associate at work or in social life, instead of aiming selfishly at making all things pivot upon your likes and dislikes.

∞

Be sensitive to temperament

Knowledge of temperamental differences is useful for avoiding friction. If you want to get along well with people, you must have much good will and solid virtue. But you must also use common sense and intelligence. In any group of people, there is a wide variation in likes and dislikes and attitudes toward life. Everyone differs in temperament.

Temperament is the combination of qualities in you that makes you the kind of person you are by nature. Your temperament might

---

[96] Acts 4:32.

be called the raw material out of which you must forge a strong character. There are both good and bad points in each temperament. Strive to overcome the bad tendencies of your particular temperament and to bring out the good qualities of which others' temperaments are capable.

∞

Strive for a balanced degree of sensitivity

Oversensitiveness is often a source of friction in human relationships. To be sensitive is good, but to let oneself grow overly sensitive causes unhappiness.

People of a certain type of temperament cannot help being sensitive. Some by nature appear well armored against the disappointments of life. But there are others who by nature are highly sensitive and are inclined to be introspective and melancholic. It is very easy for them to recognize slights, even sometimes where they do not exist. They are inclined to brood over these real or imagined slights, with the result that they make themselves and those around them miserable.

There is no disgrace in the fact that a person is endowed with a sensitive temperament. A vivid imagination and delicately balanced feelings and emotions make it possible for one to appreciate to a high degree beauty and goodness. If you are sensitive, your task is to bring out the best in your temperament and to be on your guard against the growth of evil tendencies. You must make a valiant effort to avoid brooding over real or imagined slights. Do not let your natural tendency to introspection become exaggerated; force yourself into a healthy, active association with others. Be devoted to prayer.

If you are not sensitive, then you must exercise patience. Every temperament has its faults, and patience on the part of all will reduce friction. You may never reach perfect charity, but at least you can constantly make new beginnings and thereby cut friction down to a minimum. You and others will be much happier, for the result will be unity of thought, without which true charity is impossible.

∽

See yourself and others as you are

Charity requires humility. St. Paul exhorts the Philippians to be unselfish and lowly in mind when he says, "Let nothing be done through contention, neither by vainglory; but in humility, let each esteem others better than themselves, each one not considering the things that are his own, but those that are other men's. For let this mind be in you, which was also in Christ Jesus."[97]

Pride stands in the way of self-effacing charity. It is hard for a self-centered and self-seeking disposition to yield to others. You must strike at pride, the root of the evil that harms charity so much. You may recognize its subtle workings in your refusing to adapt yourself to others in lawful things, in your considering yourself superior to others, and in protecting your interests to the exclusion of those of others.

Humility holds in check your inordinate striving for greatness and esteem. It is an indispensable prerequisite for genuine charity. There are some people who bitterly resent the kind of treatment that they frequently hand out to others. The practical joker seems to be happiest when he is putting something over on somebody else, often to the extent of making that somebody else appear the fool, with fake telephone calls, impersonations, and tricks. But let someone succeed in fooling him, and he is grieved and angry.

[97] Phil. 2:3-5 (Douay-Rheims edition).

The person who has a vicious tongue when it comes to talking about others, and is always ready to express a suspicion about their motives, manners, or actions, is always ready to fight for his so-called honor when anyone so much as breathes a word about him that he considers derogatory.

Then there is the person who wants to order others around, whether he has the authority to do so or not, and bitterly resents getting orders or even suggestions from others — even from his lawful superiors. Such behavior stems from a deeply rooted pride and shows inconsistency of character. These people are convinced that they have rights that others do not have and that they are much more clever, intelligent, and virtuous than others. Such pride needs to be corrected by humility.

If you are filled with a sincere reverence for everything pertaining to God and your neighbor, you will not appropriate to yourself more than is your due. This is true humility.

If you consider your own sins, how can you have an exalted opinion of yourself? It is not enough just to tell yourself that you are a sinner, like all men. Think of those certain sins that you are especially ashamed to admit even to yourself and for which you are genuinely sorry. If you admit them to God, even in the privacy of your heart, it will be impossible for you to be upset because of the wrongs you have to endure from others. Anger will melt away, revenge will disappear, and you will humbly accept every slight or injury in expiation for your sins. Such prayerful pondering of your own sins will make you truly humble of heart and mind.

∞

Attribute your good works to God
When you perform any kind deed, do not speak of it to others. If you do, its heavenly influence over you may disappear. Do not

dwell upon your kind actions in your own mind either. Such actions were the result of the influence of grace.

When you are tempted to be complacent about your kind actions, think rather of God's goodness to mankind, remember His sanctity and power, and you will be ashamed. This will help you to keep yourself within the limits of your own littleness. When people thank you, accept their thanks politely, but think of God, to whom all praise is due.

∞

Regard your neighbor as better than you

Humility urges you to consider and treat your neighbor as your superior, that is, as having a better standing with God than you have. St. Paul would have all "in humility . . . esteem others better than themselves." If you are imbued with this thought, you can scarcely become angry on account of seeming ill-treatment that you may receive from your neighbor. You will not be contentious. Difference of opinion may exist, but it will not occasion unworthy behavior. If such esteem exists mutually in a group of persons, no really painful situations will arise and no one will take offense at the other. The result will be a beautiful concord.

Be modest in the estimation of yourself. St. Paul exhorts all of us: "I, therefore, a prisoner for the Lord, beg you to lead a life worthy of the calling to which you have been called."[98] Such an attitude of mind is not pious exaggeration, nor is it likely to produce an inferiority complex. None of us is in a position to know truly how we stand in the omniscience of God. It may be only too true that your neighbor has been more faithful to grace than you, more generous to God and more zealous in charity than you.

[98] Eph. 4:1.

∞

Be unselfish

Humility demands unselfishness. It is noble and holy to be mindful of others and to do them good. St. Paul insists on that other-regarding quality of charity, "Let each of you look not only to his own interests, but also to the interests of others."

Looking after your own good is not condemnable, since charity begins at home, but it should not stop there. Proper self-love is the norm of brotherly love, for we are told to love our neighbor as ourselves. But exclusive consideration of self is to be censured.

St. Paul says, "Let this mind be in you, which was also in Christ Jesus." To aim at likeness to the mind of Christ is not only a noble ambition, but also a tremendous privilege. If you consider "the mind of Christ" toward you — how He has looked to your interests in every circumstance of your life when He might so easily have let justice take its course — you ought to be most willing to be humble in mind when dealing with your fellowmen.

Ask our Lord for the virtue of humility, that your charity may be genuine. He said of Himself, "Take my yoke upon you, and learn of me, because I am meek and humble of heart."[99]

∞

Show consideration for others

Considerateness implies that you prefer others to yourself. It is a genuine virtue because it is sincere charity, a fulfillment of the command of our Lord: "Love your neighbor as yourself."[100]

Considerateness is an unpretentious virtue. It is queenly charity wearing her humblest garb, so she often remains unrecognized.

[99] Matt. 11:29 (Douay-Rheims edition).
[100] Matt. 22:39.

106

If you render some service or forgive injuries, you will earn gratitude and admiration. But if you are considerate toward others, you will seldom hear yourself praised. Considerate people make a point of practicing this virtue in such a way that it benefits many, but catches the eye of only a few.

Considerate love, with an air about it that inspires reverence, shows itself, for the most part, in the little things of life. But often a person will find it harder to do trifles than heroic actions. Even if these trifles were only of little account, they would still stand for something really great because considerateness finds its opportunity almost at every hour of the day.

You can show consideration by avoiding useless and annoying noise, such as slamming doors, walking heavily, talking, laughing, or singing boisterously when others are trying to rest or work. Such conduct betrays not only thoughtlessness, but also a weakness of character, a lack of the finer qualities that characterize a generous soul. Such practices may be motivated by the vain and perverted desire to draw attention to oneself, or to disturb others for the sake of petty revenge or dislike.

Consideration for others is a most necessary virtue. Perhaps mankind's greatest pain is caused less by the blind elements such as sickness and accidents, than by a lack of consideration for one another. Lack of consideration is responsible for an immense amount of humiliation, suffering, discord, and lawsuits.

You are not benefitting mankind very much if, in one place, you cause a small amount of human happiness, but elsewhere you cause great unhappiness by being inconsiderate. What is the good of giving valuable gifts to friends at Christmas if you spoil many of their hours in the course of the year by harshness?

Even if your considerate love is not recognized by people, God sees and hears and will also reward one day the words that you left unsaid, the unkind remarks that you repressed, and the wishes that you gave up. He will also deal considerately with your weaknesses and your unfulfilled aspirations. But if you are not in the habit of practicing considerateness, how can you expect consideration from God?

∞

Strive to suffer graciously

Considerateness implies that you suffer graciously. Kind suffering is a form of kind deeds. If you need the help of grace to perform a kind deed, you are even more in need of grace to suffer kindly.

One of the most attractive features of holiness is to combine suffering with gentleness. This demands that suffering be almost wholly influenced by supernatural grace.

What is more beautiful than considerateness for others when you yourself are unhappy? Such charity leaves a deep impression and makes others more gentle. On the other hand, it is very unkind to communicate your sadness to others. Sometimes you may have a sickly appetite for sympathy that will not let you keep your tiny sorrows to yourself.

Kind suffering will make you look at what others feel rather than at what you have to bear. You will see your own crosses on other people's shoulders, and consequently you will be all the more kind to them. The saints were silent in suffering, because they knew that what they suffered was itself a suffering to those who loved them.

Make an effort to hide your pains and sorrows. But, while you do so, let them also urge you to be kind and cheerful to those around you. The very darkness within you should create a sunshine around you. In this way, the spirit of Jesus will take possession of your soul.

∞

Learn the ways to practice considerateness

The following suggestions will help you to practice considerateness toward others:

• *Ask yourself some personal questions.* Put yourself in the place of the other person. If you were in his place, how would the thing in question appear to you? How would you judge it? How would you feel if what you now hear about another were said about you? What would you wish others to say and think of you?

Put yourself in the place of the person's mother, or someone else dear to him. How would his mother judge the matter? What would she wish? What would she do?

Think of God. How does the other person stand in His eyes? What is God's viewpoint? What does God want of the person? What does God want of you now?

Frank answers to questions such as these will lead you to honesty in any situation. You will see at once what you must think and say, since you must love and treat everyone else like yourself. These questions reveal how selfish you really are without intending to be and how quick and superficial your judgments can be.

• *Remember the good points and virtues of others.* A person who is kind never sees personal weaknesses in others. Kindness is the eye that overlooks your friend's broken gateway, but sees a rose that blossoms in his garden. There is nothing that will so manifest your character, your heart, and your soul as this sweet graciousness.

Dwell frequently in thought on the good traits of those for whom you may have natural aversions, so that you may acquire the habit of seeing only the good or the commendable in them. Their virtues usually outweigh their faults. If you do this, then unkindness, aloofness, suspicion, rash judgments, envy, detraction, and slander will not find a place in your life.

Make allowances for human shortcomings. The undesirable or the evil in any human life is not the whole of that person. No one is wholly bad; few are wholly good. Faults are in most cases the weaknesses attendant upon great strengths. Judge a man not by his failures, but by what he makes of them. With a little good will, you can recognize and appreciate the good in others and show it respect. It is Christlike to forget the rest.

• *Remember your own faults.* When you recognize a tendency to judge others uncharitably, you ought to scrutinize your own actions to find out in how far you have been failing in similar cases. Your own faults may be greater than those you condemn in others. The words of the Scriptures apply here: "Physician, heal yourself."[101] Be determined to correct the unfair tendency. This acknowledgment of your weakness will produce some good results. Serious, persevering prayer will secure God's grace for you to support your will.

• *Do not be curious regarding the life or actions of others.* Our Lord's words to Peter when he inquired into the manner of John's death — "What is that to you? Follow me."[102] — is a clear-cut answer of Divine Wisdom relative to your judging

[101] Luke 4:23.
[102] John 21:22.

the life or actions of others. Remember the Savior's words to those who accused the woman caught in adultery: "Let him who is without sin among you be the first to throw a stone at her."[103]

St. Ignatius Loyola once wrote: "The man who sets about making others better is wasting his time, unless he begins with himself." This does not mean that you have to be perfect in all things before trying to help others. But it does mean that you should acknowledge your own faults and strive to correct them, even while you try to do your part in winning the world back to Christ. The more perfect you are, the more gentle you become toward the defects of others.

With so much in your life that needs correction, you have enough to do to mind your own business. You will be blessed if, at the end of your life, you have all your accounts straight with God, let alone trying to regulate the lives of others. In the book of Tobit, we read, "And what you hate, do not do to anyone."[104] You are truly charitable when your first principle is to cause others as little pain as possible. That is considerate love.

∞

Exercise patience

Charity requires patience. St. Thomas Aquinas summarizes the wonderful effects of patience in these words: "Patience is said to make work perfect, by bearing with adversities: from these proceed first, sadness, which patience moderates; and secondly, anger, which meekness moderates; thirdly, hatred, which charity takes

---

[103] John 8:7.
[104] Tob. 4:15.

away; and fourthly, revenge or the infliction of unjust damage, which justice forbids."

∞

Consider others' patience toward you

St. Paul says, "Bear one another's burdens, and so fulfill the law of Christ."[105] The law of Christ is: "Love one another as I have loved you."[106] The advice to "bear one another's burdens" refers to patience. The apostle gives us a very gentle yet unmistakable hint at why we should patiently bear with troublesome people. He suggests that we ourselves may be burdensome.

It is good to be reminded of this fact, because we do not easily think of it. We do not feel the weight of the burden we lay on the shoulders of others. People perhaps do not say a word about how troublesome you are, but they bear with you in kindly silence and patience. Hence, you should repay them in the same way, rewarding patience with patience by putting up with what may be troublesome in them.

Examine your conscience from time to time to see what there is in your nature, your conduct, and your actions that may get on the nerves of those around you. There are very few people who please everybody in every way. When you have discovered your defects, do what you can to correct them.

∞

Shoulder your part of the world's cross

The chief reason for patience is pointed out in the second half of the apostle's advice: "and so fulfill the law of Christ." The law of

---

[105] Gal. 6:2.
[106] John 15:12.

Christ is not only the law of charity, but also the law of self-sacrifice. Our Lord said, "If any man would come after me, let him deny himself and take up his cross daily and follow me."[107] What the apostle calls a burden, Christ describes as a cross. Since God Himself deliberately places your neighbor at your side, and since He Himself laid the burden of this cross upon you, you must look upon another's burden as "your cross" and bear it as your own personal cross. Let our Lord be your example. The burdens of others became His Cross. The prophet says, "Surely He has borne our griefs."[108]

All of us are sometimes burdensome to God. What would become of you if a feeling of aversion for you could arise in His heart? What if He were to lose patience with you?

An old eastern legend tells the story of a stranger who sought shelter for the night in another's tent. He awoke in the middle of the night and, becoming impatient because he could not sleep, blasphemed God. Awakened by the stranger's profanity, the scandalized tent owner drove the man from his home. In the morning, an angel is said to have appeared to him, exclaiming: "I sent a stranger to you for shelter. Where is he?" "I would not let him stay," explained the owner, "because he blasphemed God." "For forty years," replied the angel, "God has been patient with that man. For one single night could you not bear with him?"

You may be sure that God will go on bearing with you. Thank the Lord for bearing your burdens, your sins, and your troublesomeness. Then rise and shoulder a small part of the burden of the Cross; that is, bear with the weaknesses of the people around you, and so accompany, like Simon of Cyrene, the divine Cross-bearer,

[107] Luke 9:23.
[108] Isa. 53:4.

in fulfillment of His command: "A new commandment I give to you, that you love one another; even as I have loved you, that you also love one another."[109] Only if you fulfill the law that our Lord gave us by His own example, and become like Christ in love for your neighbor, do you have a just claim to call yourself a Christian.

The practice of patience toward one another, the overlooking of one another's defects, and the bearing of one another's burdens is the most elementary condition of all human social activity in the family, in the professions, and in society. St. Francis de Sales says, "Men must have patience with one another, and the bravest are those who put up the best with the imperfections of their fellowmen."

The art of bearing one another's burdens is difficult to attain for poor human nature, but, when once attained, is productive of much peace of mind and heart, both for self and others. This art requires much humility and proved loyalty to Christ.

∞

Train yourself in patience

We all cannot and do not think alike. Human prudence should make you realize that it is easier and more profitable to bear with others than to expect them to change habits of many years' standing to accommodate you. Personal experience should help you to understand that others sincerely regret that they are subject to distressing defects. Why not be patient and forgiving?

The following suggestions may help you to practice patience:

• *Look for or presume excusing causes.* Although you should never condone wrongdoing, try to find or presume excusing

[109] John 13:34.

causes, for the erring person may have been completely overtaken by strong temptation or may lack the necessary understanding of the seriousness of his actions. You must have your eyes open to the whole truth, lest hasty judgments and prejudices close them to a part of the truth. This was the spirit of the Savior on the Cross when He prayed, "Father, forgive them; for they know not what they do."[110]

It is simple humanity not to scrutinize too severely the offenses of others, so that, in turn, others may bear with you. If each of us assumes the right to investigate the shortcomings of others, nothing will be done as it ought to be done; only constant bickering and strife will result. On the other hand, where there is patience, forbearance, and mutual sharing of the burdens of life, there the burdens are reciprocally lightened.

Your natural proneness to think harshly of others and deal rigidly with them is inconsistency on your part, because in your own failings you make fine discriminations and most polite considerations that you are reluctant to supply to the actions of others.

If you use the standards God must apply to you, you will find yourself seriously deficient in many respects. Most of us have plenty to do to "sweep before our own doors" without bothering about the particles on the threshold of a neighbor. St. Paul exhorts us in these words: "With patience, forbear one another in love."[111]

Judging leniently and compassionately the weakness and probable ignorance of others may forestall the repetition of

[110] Luke 23:34.
[111] Cf. Eph. 4:2.

an undesirable act or word. The true spirit of charity must animate you, and that is nothing less than Christ's spirit of the forgiveness and expiation of sins.

• *Forgive injuries.* God's conduct toward you is regulated by your conduct toward your neighbor. Jesus said, "For with the judgment you pronounce you will be judged, and the measure you give will be the measure you get."[112]

Jesus enters into details by saying that His Father will forgive your sins only if you forgive those offenses which are committed against you. Unless you show mercy, you can look forward to a judgment without mercy. If you do not want to be judged or condemned, do not judge or condemn. If you want God to show kindness toward you, be kind to your neighbor. "Give, and it will be given to you; good measure, pressed down, shaken together, running over will be put into your lap."[113]

The duty of forgiving is so necessary that our Lord said, "So if you are offering your gift at the altar, and there remember that your brother has something against you, leave your gift there before the altar and go; first be reconciled to your brother, and then come and offer your gift."[114]

The first gift you must offer God is a heart free from all resentment toward others. Don't ask yourself whether the person involved is more in the wrong than you are, or whether he should take the first step. As soon as possible, clear up every misunderstanding by an honest explanation. If the other person is the first to present his excuses, forgive

[112] Matt. 7:2.
[113] Luke 6:38.
[114] Matt. 5:23-24.

116

him at once, for our Lord said, "If you forgive men their trespasses, your heavenly Father also will forgive you; but if you do not forgive men their trespasses, neither will your Father forgive your trespasses."[115]

If you desire to obtain from God the pardon of the sins you have committed against Him, you must forgive from your heart those who have offended you. What is more, you must pray for them even as Jesus did. This is the greatest act of charity.

• *Bear injustice patiently.* When it pleases God to permit you to labor under the cloud of false suspicion, false judgment, calumny, or detraction, try to remember the following suggestions:

• *Try to see God's permission of the happening.* St. Francis de Sales gives this advice: "We must have patience not only to be ill, but to be ill with the illness which God wills, in the place where He wills, and among such persons as He wills; and so of our tribulations." Try to avoid thinking of the grievance. "Love is patient."[116] Concentrating on wrongs done to you generally impresses the undesirable facts more deeply on your memory and does not obviate the evil. Complete abandonment to God and trust in His Providence form the most worthy procedure for your soul.

• *Do not talk the matter over with others* except for the purpose of getting direction to make virtue out of necessity. Other persons seldom understand adequately. St. Ignatius Loyola says, "If we do not feel in ourselves a perfect patience,

[115] Matt. 6:14-15.
[116] 1 Cor. 13:4.

we have great reason rather to complain of the sensuality of our flesh, of our being neither mortified nor dead to the things of the world, as we ought to be, than to accuse those who load us with insults and ignominy." Learn to bear snubs, setbacks, and sharp tongues nobly with Christ at Herod's court. Justice will prevail. God will right all wrongs, if not in this life, then surely at the Last Judgment.

• *Let this cross be a source of self-sanctification* rather than torture for your soul. Offer the pain you must suffer in expiation for sin — your own as well as those of others — and also for blessings upon those who have been unfair to you.

• *Find strength and consolation in prayer.* You need God's grace to make any difficulty a means of greater personal holiness. Prayer secures that grace. You can conquer anything with God's grace, but nothing without it. Your prayer need not be long, but brief and definite. Take time to pray for the interests of Christ and His Church persecuted in so many countries today. Pray for the checking of the moral evils so prevalent even among Catholics.

• *Pray for the grace of conversion for failing ones.* Unless the erring are incorrigibly obstinate or hopelessly blind, they will, by the grace of God, be brought to a salutary realization of their wrongdoing through patience on your part.

• *Cultivate the devotion of reparation to the Sacred Heart.* Ask Jesus, the forbearing and long-suffering Savior, for a tolerant frame of mind regarding the actions of others. Ask Him for the power to influence others, especially through your example, to put aside their undesirable habits. Ask for the grace to remember that others exercise much patience with you. Especially, ask Jesus crucified for a practical and more perfect understanding of His great example in forgiving, so that you may learn to bear with others.

∞

Sympathy shows your likeness to God

There is much and varied misery in this vale of tears, and every kind of need calls for help. The anguish of human suffering moves the heart of God and His angels. "He is good, for His steadfast love endures forever," says Holy Scripture.[117] God's mercy is ever busy relieving the misery that man has brought, and daily brings, upon himself and into the world in which he dwells.

St. Paul speaks of God in these words: "Blessed be the God and Father of our Lord Jesus Christ, the Father of mercies and God of all comfort, who comforts us in our affliction, so that we may be able to comfort those who are in any affliction, with the comfort which we ourselves are comforted by God."[118]

God gave you gifts to aid you in striving after kindness of heart. He made you in His own image and likeness, and He is love. In Baptism He gave you, together with sanctifying grace, the virtues of faith, hope, and charity. Inasmuch as you are a child of God, your soul finds it easy and almost natural to embrace in its love God, the Creator. St. Paul speaks of this in these words: "God's love has been poured into our hearts through the Holy Spirit who has been given to us."[119]

In spite of the havoc wrought in his being, the natural man still retains in his soul some traces of God's glory. Every human heart

[117] 2 Chron. 7:3.
[118] 2 Cor. 1:3-4.
[119] Rom. 5:5.

has a bent toward sociability and friendship. Closely linked to this yearning is your soul's desire to enjoy pleasure and beauty not alone, but in the company of others. And as you feel a natural desire to let others have part in your happiness, you derive new joy from the act of sharing with them.

Strongest of all is your natural gift of sympathy. Even rude and rough men often feel sympathy when they witness another's pain. Through the instinct of sympathy, nature prompts all to help those in danger and to relieve from pain those who suffer. Sympathy is a sacred remnant of the primeval likeness to Himself in which the merciful and compassionate Lord of the universe created us in the beginning.

∞

Answer the call to show sympathy

The God of all comfort wills that angels and men cooperate with Him in the fulfillment of the promise: "Blessed are those who mourn, for they shall be comforted."[120] Even as God sent an angel to comfort His Son when He was sorrowful even unto death,[121] so you are sent to comfort some sorrowful child of God. St. Paul says, "We exhort you, brethren, admonish the idle, encourage the faint-hearted, help the weak, be patient with them all. See that none of you repays evil for evil, but always seek to do good to one another and to all."[122]

God gave you the faculty of sympathy, which enables you to recognize the pleading of hidden, silent want and the misery of suffering that cannot speak. Sympathy will not let you go thoughtlessly

---

[120] Matt. 5:4.
[121] Cf. Matt. 26:38; Luke 22:43.
[122] 1 Thess. 5:14-15.

past those in need, but will prompt you to offer your help. And unless you do offer help, your life will be selfish and meaningless. If you do what you can to lessen human misery, you are God's helper and you have discovered a most beautiful calling, for to be always ready to help is truly the vocation of God's own children.

The following suggestions may help you to be sympathetic:

* *Love your neighbor for the sake of God.* This will lift your kindness to a supernatural plane and, at the same time, make it more generous, active, and universal.

* *Try to see Jesus Christ in your neighbor.* Love for your neighbor means loving God in your neighbor. Our Lord identifies Himself with your neighbor and considers whatever service you render to others as rendered to Himself. He also refers to kind thoughts when He says, "Truly I say to you, as you did it to one of the least of these my brethren, you did it to me."[123] Your motto should be: "Christ in all!"

* *Interest yourself in others.* Take a sincere interest in all that concerns them, as St. Paul admonishes, "Rejoice with those who rejoice; weep with those who weep."[124]

* *Offer consolation and prayer* if you cannot give help or counsel. To comfort a human heart is a holy service and a sacred duty. When your heart is moved by genuine sympathy, often a few words will be enough to soothe your neighbor's pain.

* *Do not refuse to carry out your vocation of helper.* If you remain deaf to the cry for help, you will not be able to face

[123] Matt. 25:40.
[124] Rom. 12:15.

God. If you refuse others your help, how can you dare to call for God's help?

How unfortunate it would be if Christians — all of whom ought to be angels of comfort — were unwilling to offer comfort! Christ, who so often spoke a gentle "Do not weep!"[125] did not remain uncomforted in His own darkest hours. If you gladly comfort others, you will also behold some ray of light and consolation in your own misery.

Christ, the man of sorrows,[126] whose heart was oppressed with anguish and grief, is the best of all comforters. He invites all: "Come to me, all who labor and are heavy laden, and I will give you rest."[127]

[125] Luke 7:13, 8:52.
[126] Isa. 53:3.
[127] Matt. 11:28.

∞

Chapter Eight

Discover the transforming power of kind thoughts

Kind thoughts give power to words and works. Without kind thoughts, there can be no charity. The kind thought is the mold into which charity is cast. The thought eventually takes shape in words and works of charity, but it remains always the quickening power of these words and works, giving them their beauty, life, and worth, as in the case of the widow's mite.[128] The kind thought constitutes the most precious element of even the greatest works of charity.

Thoughts are forces; they are the great sources of power. Even the mighty words and works of love of God Himself — the word by which He called the world into being and created a soul to share His own bliss, the tremendous work of the Incarnation and the death of His own Son upon a Cross — are to be traced to the kindly thoughts of a loving heart.

Whenever the loving thought does not accompany words and works of charity, these are dead. And every man who does not cherish within him kind and loving thoughts — whatever his

[128] Cf. Mark 12:41-44.

works or words may be — is devoid of charity, and, on the authority of St. John, such a one is dead: "He who does not love remains in death."[129]

∞

Kind thoughts help you deal successfully with others

As a mother's love draws the heart of her child like a powerful magnet, so, too, does the genuinely kind person wield the power to influence others for good. Only a kind person is able to judge another justly and to make allowances for his weaknesses. A kind eye, while recognizing defects, sees beyond them. Its gaze is like that of a gentle mother who judges her beloved child more leniently, and at the same time more correctly, than a stranger would.

No one ever saw human weakness more clearly than Jesus saw it in His apostles. Yet how patient He was with their worldliness, their faults! The wellspring of His patience was a kindness of heart that nothing could disturb. His followers clung to Him with an unshakable confidence. Love radiated from His person and warmed the hearts of those surrounding Him. Nevertheless, on occasion He could show a firmness that nothing could weaken. Never did He waver or compromise when the glory of His Father or the salvation of souls was at stake.

Whenever your soul cherishes a gracious thought, it is as if God sees His own Being reflected in a silent, sacred likeness. A kind thought is like the image of the Savior in your soul. God beholds it and rejoices at it and blesses your soul because your thoughts and sentiments are so much after His own Heart.

Character is both formed and influenced in the world of your thoughts. If you are master in your thoughts, you are master

[129] 1 John 3:14.

everywhere. If you have learned to control your thoughts, you have yourself completely under control. If you have a kind heart, your words and deeds will also be kind. If you fostered more kind thoughts, you would necessarily be richer also in kind deeds. It must, therefore, be very important to cultivate kind thoughts.

∞

Kind thoughts preserve you from many sins against charity

The practice of kind thoughts has an effect on your spiritual life. It leads to self-denial. The practice of kind thoughts enables you to overcome criticism and all the influence it may exert on others. You thereby sacrifice successes at the moment they are within your reach. The triumph over a proud heart and a bitter temper is the result of difficult spiritual combat, but it brings its re-ward, for self-denial is a fountain of peace and joy in your soul.

The practice of kind thoughts is your main help to that com-plete control of the tongue without which all religion is vain, as St. James says.[130] The interior beauty of your soul through habitual kindness of thought is greater than words can describe.

The practice of kind thoughts helps you to grow in the spiritual life. It opens and smooths the paths of prayer. It sheds a clear, still light over your self-knowledge and enables you to find God easily.

Kind thoughts imply a contact with God and have a special power to let in upon you the light of God. They are the scent with which the creature is penetrated through the indwelling of the Creator.

Charity is the deepest view of life, because it is nearest to God's view. This is the reverse of a worldly and superficial view of things. God's view is not merely the truest view, but the only view that is

[130] James 1:26.

true at all. Thus, uncharitable judgments and prejudices, misunderstandings and suspicions, envy and jealousy, and uncharitable words and slander will not take root in a soul that thinks kind thoughts. Aversions and bitterness disappear, strained relations are smoothed out, and petty arguments end of themselves.

If you were to make it a practice to begin each day with benevolent thoughts in your heart, instead of selfish ambition, you would not be inclined to deny a helping hand or ignore a favor rendered you. You would certainly be disposed to spare the feelings of oversensitive persons, to sympathize with the suffering, and to help others in the solution of vexing problems confronting them. If, instead of harsh thoughts and bitter resentment, you fostered in your heart a readiness to forgive and forget, you would not find it too difficult to adopt a friendly attitude toward those who are habitually cold and hostile toward you.

To keep firmly to supernatural principles in your daily conduct is not easy. It takes great willpower to master thoughts of hatred, selfishness, and mistrust that rush in upon you and to turn them into gracious and kind thoughts. You need God's grace and much self-discipline to realize the ideal expressed in the words of St. Paul: "Put on, then, as God's chosen ones, holy and beloved, compassion, kindness, lowliness, meekness, and patience."[131]

Get into the habit of putting a kind interpretation on all you see and hear, and of having kind thoughts of everyone of whom you think. This will enable you to live a new life in a new world.

Compare it to your state in Heaven someday. One very important feature of Heaven will be the absence of all bitterness and criticism and the possession of thoughts of the most tender kindness. Thus, by cultivating kind thoughts, you are in a very special

[131] Col. 3:12.

way preparing for Heaven. You are actually earning Heaven. By God's grace, you are imitating in your own mind that upon which, in the Divine Mind, you rest all your hopes — merciful judgments, favorable interpretations, thoughts of kindness, and tolerant compassion.

Kind thoughts imply a great deal of thinking about others according to a divine ideal — the ideal of charity. By sweetening the fountains of your thoughts, you destroy the bitterness of your judgments. And if you are habitually kind in thought through supernatural motives, you are far on the way to becoming a saint.

∞

Kind thoughts promote peace

Whatever man craves or does, he does for the purpose of securing peace. A man's face is troubled, his work hindered, and his whole life made miserable whenever he is at variance with himself, with God, or with a fellowman. But as soon as he has recovered the peace he had lost, his face glows, his spirit revives, and his heart is full of the joy of life. The peace of the supernatural world has its source in the very heart of God. The highest bliss that God has prepared for us is everlasting peace, "the peace . . . which passes all understanding."[132] The everlasting home of God's children is called Jerusalem, that is, "the City of Peace."

Christ said, "Blessed are the peacemakers, for they shall be called sons of God."[133] The word used by our Lord when He uttered the Beatitudes designates not only those who are peace-loving, but also those who procure peace. This is one of the most splendid duties of Christian charity.

[132] Phil. 4:7.
[133] Matt. 5:9.

To keep peace in your hearts, you must cultivate kind thoughts. Such thoughts are the origin of kind words and deeds, which bring peace to the hearts of men. The more peace-loving you are, the more powerful you are as a peacemaker. You do not make peace with your tongue; your whole person brings about peace. When a person is out of harmony with God, there is no more beautiful work of charity than to reconcile him to his Creator. The warring world can recover peace only through Christian charity.

If you are really kind, you will always fear lest you destroy another's peace. You will prefer to forgo some trifling right, to bear some small imposition or slight offense, to turn a deaf ear to an unjust remark, or to renounce having the last word, rather than to start an argument. Still less will you disturb another's peace in matters in which you are not concerned. You will not approve the conduct of one who selfishly exploits another, and you will refrain from inciting the one against the other. When you hear a person speaking unkindly of another behind his back, you will carefully avoid relating what you have heard to the person talked about because it is wrong to disturb the mutual harmony between two people.

Your spiritual poverty may prevent you from sharing the power of the saints and their influence as peacemakers. If you succeed in bringing together and reconciling only a few men, you, too, will be a true child of your heavenly Father, and your reward will be to hear yourself called "blessed" by Christ Himself.

St. Margaret Mary says, "Our Lord wishes us to have great charity for our neighbor, for whom we should pray as for ourselves; it is one of the characteristic effects of this devotion [to the Sacred Heart] to reconcile hearts and to bring peace to souls."

Genuine love will always feel urged to communicate joy — to be a joy-giver. Mankind needs joy. In our own day, the world is particularly sick because of its joylessness, and all its noisy amusements can neither hide nor drive away its misery. Genuine love always feels impelled to listen to this hunger of the human soul for love.

∞

Kind thoughts never fail to bring joy

You may have performed splendid deeds, but you will surely fail to achieve happiness if your actions have not been inspired by love. A simple loving thought can dispel the clouds of depression, discontent, and sadness; but if your thoughts are kindly, you are indeed a happy person.

Kind thoughts radiate light and gladness among men. They gladden you first and then those around you. People never fail to notice the presence of such thoughts. Maybe they read your thoughts upon your face, see them in your eyes, or hear them in the tone of your voice. They are able to feel and to recognize the kindness that gladdens their hearts.

In order to give joy to others, you must first possess it yourself. In the heart of Jesus, there reigned a deep, holy joy, in spite of all the tragedy and sadness that marked His career. The night before His death He said, "These things I have spoken to you, that my joy may be in you, and that your joy may be full."[134]

Your religion, the true religion of joy, helps you to be a joy-giver. God is the source of all joy. Through prayer and the sacraments, you draw close to God. Draw true joy from the heart of God, and then pass it from your heart into other hearts during your day's work among your fellowmen. When you have entered into eternity, you will be amazed on realizing what a wonderful

---

[134] John 15:11.

kingdom of joy you might have set up around you on earth by means of mere trifles.

And if it should happen that no one is aware of the pearls of kindly thoughts enclosed in your heart, so that no one rejoices over them, God, who knows all things and who is Himself an eternal thought of love, is aware of them. He rejoices over them. When you cherish a gracious thought, it is as if God saw His own Being reflected in a silent, sacred likeness, as the stars are reflected in a crystal pool.

The essence of love depends on union, and union with God and your neighbor brings joy. The love of God is an incomparable source of joy. All the beauty of the whole world is a gift by which God seeks to give us joy. The sense of God's nearness is but a joyful gift of God to His creatures. God's love and human love are bliss poured out upon the world to fill it with a foretaste of Heaven.

It usually costs little to bring joy to another's heart. All it takes is a little good will, a trifling exertion for the sake of your neighbor, a cheering gift, a few words, and sometimes just a smile.

A friend rejoices in the presence of his friend, but love can transcend time and space and produce a spiritual nearness when bodily presence is denied. Even in this life, there is joy for the heart that loves God. The love of God brings Him to the soul in an intimacy of union that is full of joy. In the Beatific Vision, that joy will be "what no eye has seen, nor ear heard."[135]

∞

Kind thoughts let you share in the good that others do
God gives us our gifts, our talents, and our tasks, not only for our own good and our own happiness, but also for the benefit of

---

[135] 1 Cor. 2:9.

others who share them with us. No one of us is sufficient to himself. Only an omnipotent man could live without the help of the talents of others. Since we need one another and one another's work, the very need should bring us closer together.

Not all members of God's family can be priests or sisters or brothers. Not all can be married. Not all have a special talent that may be used for God and man in a single state. Yet the whole family of God needs priests and sisters and brothers and married people and single people. It needs the men who conceive and plan and direct, just as it needs the men who do the physical work. This mutual need should give us a sense of appreciative gratitude for all the work of all the men on whom we must rely. That is the reason for the words of the psalmist: "Behold how good and pleasant it is when brothers dwell in unity."[136]

Basically we all have one vocation. St. Paul puts it in these words: "It is my prayer that you may be pure and blameless for the day of Christ, filled with the fruits of righteousness which come through Jesus Christ, to the glory and praise of God."[137] That is the purpose of every creature.

Your vocation in life is doing your own task well. Once you learn to see God's will in the design, you come to realize that the offering of a stenographer's life can be as pleasing to God as the offering of a doctor's life or a priest's life.

The good actions of others may be yours in the sight of God if, when you notice them, you offer them to God with a prayer and good wishes. You cooperate in God's work when you wish your neighbor well, when you implore God's blessing on his work, and rejoice and thank God for another's success. You will become

[136] Ps. 133:1.
[137] Cf. Phil. 1:9-11.

aware how blind you have been not to have realized the far-reaching effects of an encouraging word, a friendly glance, or a kind deed. The good that you do in this way will be rewarded more than any other because it is wholly selfless.

Although you cannot carry out certain works of charity, your soul is a garden in which you may plant the fairest flowers of loving thoughts. Especially at prayer, when grace is most ready to assist your efforts, try to weed out all bitter memories, all severe judgments, all suspicions, and all resentful and angry thoughts, and in their stead plant in the rich soil of your soul the noble sentiments of charity. Carefully cherish and tend these gentle thoughts so that they may thrive and fill your day with their perfume. Try to fill the whole of this present life with such thoughts, and you will not only do good to those around you, but you will also share in the good that others do.

Be cooperative with associates. Good principles and justice must be evident in all your relationships with others. Since ways and means of attaining ends are varied, put aside your own views, where justice is not violated, in deference to those of others. This is heroic self-denial. Through kindly interest in the work of others, and by generous cooperation with them, you become associated with their works and share in the solidarity of the Mystical Body of Christ.

Union with God and your neighbor brings peace, for the possession of charity means that all your desires and tendencies are directed to God. There is none of the irritation of domestic strife and conscious disharmony in your heart that disturbs the calm of peace. Between God and you, there is a unity of will that safeguards you against the discord of worldlings. But there is still room for that holy fear that makes you flee from sin and the judgment of God. Such fear does not drive out peace. Moreover, the love that binds you to your neighbor for the love of God secures a harmony of cooperation in the pursuit of good.

Living in peace with your fellowmen is an effect of charity — proof that you love your neighbor as yourself, that you respect his will as well as your own, and that you are minded to unite your will even at the price of self-renunciation. Thus, you not only preserve peace in your own life, but also definitely pave the way to peace in the hearts of others.

You can be one of the promoters of peace to whom Christ referred when He said: "Blessed are the peacemakers, for they shall be called sons of God." St. Paul encouraged the first Christians in these words: "[Be] eager to maintain the unity of the Spirit in the bond of peace."[138] And again, "Live in peace, and the God of love and peace will be with you."[139]

[138] Eph. 4:3.
[139] 2 Cor. 13:11.

Part Two

∞

Learn to speak kindly

∞

Chapter Nine

Dedicate yourself to truth

There is no greater source of friction than the one caused by the misuse of the tongue. The human tongue can be a very sharp and cutting instrument when powered by anger, pride, or uncharitableness. Strict control of the tongue can cut down friction and eliminate trouble.

The eighth commandment — "Thou shalt not bear false witness against thy neighbor" — calls for the conduct of trials on the plane of strict justice according to law. It not only forbids lying testimony given under oath in a court of justice or elsewhere regarding another, but it also forbids lying and unjust injury, by word or deed, of another's reputation and honor by detraction, slander, and unjust revelation of secrets.

The real evil of lying consists in the abuse of the power of speech. God gives you the power of speech to reveal the thought in your mind. When you lie, you frustrate that power in the very act of using it. You must tell the truth if you are to conform to the nature God has given you.

It is never right to abuse the power of speech, no matter what the motive may be. Everyone is bound to speak the truth on all occasions and under all circumstances. But everyone is not bound to speak out on all occasions and under all circumstances. There are times when one is bound to secrecy. But one may not keep a secret by lying.

To withhold the truth from one who is seeking information to which he has no right is lawful. When you have to keep a secret, you may use some form of words that express the veiled truth, and at the same time occasion the deception of the hearer. However, you must have a sufficiently good reason for using such broad mental restriction; moreover, you may use it only if the hearer has no right to the information he seeks. It is one thing to withhold the truth and another to utter a falsehood.

Exaggeration is a form of lying. One of the most common forms of exaggeration is that inspired by vanity. A person gives the impression by his talk that his life is full of amazing accomplishments. Another form of exaggeration is shown by the person who likes to add drama to a story. But the most dangerous and evil form of exaggeration is that in which somebody's reputation is made to suffer.

If you are given to exaggeration, you will find it a very easy way to make your friends distrust and even dislike you. Those who know you well will seldom take you seriously and will hesitate to admit you into a position of responsibility. Loose treatment of the truth can do untold harm among those who do not as yet know of your weakness. If you are given to exaggeration in speech, analyze your conversation and try to eliminate every trace of this bad habit.

∞

Avoid false pretense

False pretense is a form of lying. You are guilty of this fault if you make yourself out to be something you are not in order to impress others, to appear important, and to be admired. This is a form of vanity. You either exaggerate your standing or accomplishments or make up facts about yourself that will impress others. It is false pretense to transform a nodding acquaintance with some important person into an intimate friendship, or to boast of a glamorous past history that is largely fictional, or to be continually dropping names.

The best way to rid yourself of the habit of pretending is to cultivate simplicity and humility. Be convinced of the principle that you are what you are before God, no more and no less. You do not change your status, either in the eyes of God or of men, by self-misrepresentation in words. Rather, you lower yourself, in the eyes of both God and men, by such deceits.

Hypocrisy is the act or the habit of appearing to be one thing or to believe in one thing while in reality you are the opposite or believe in the opposite. You practice religious hypocrisy when you pretend to be a very pious and sincere Catholic, yet privately embrace some form of moral evil like adultery, birth control, or corruption in business or politics.

You practice social hypocrisy when you worm your way into the confidence of another, act as if you are solely concerned with giving sympathy and advice, draw out secrets of a personal nature, and then use the information to hurt the one whose confidence you have gained; or when you pretend to be unselfishly interested in advancing some good cause — charity, religion, or public welfare — but you have the intention of using the cause, and others who are working for it, to your own advantage.

You practice professional hypocrisy when, in public office or in business, you speak against some evil and in reality practice it yourself, or when you complain of losing money while you yourself are making an unjust profit.

It is not hypocrisy to conceal and suppress the antipathies and bitter feelings you may have toward others. You are practicing virtue if you suppress these bitter feelings not only in the presence of the people you dislike but in their absence as well.

To be outspoken when truth is under attack, when charity is being bruised, or when important issues of life are at stake is a good and courageous thing. To be outspoken when nothing is at stake except the feelings of someone else is a small and contemptible thing. A certain amount of candor in expressing your opinion is a charming thing, but it can be pushed too far. There is no virtuous necessity for expressing all the dislikes that flash across your feelings. Very often it is necessary as a matter of virtue to spare others the hurt that would be given by freely expressing your opinion.

Confusion of tact with hypocrisy leads to many equally vicious things, such as detraction, backbiting, hatred, and revenge. There is no hypocrisy in kindness, good will, charity, and forgiveness, even though these virtues run directly contrary to your feelings and inclinations.

Ordinarily lies told in jest or those told to obtain some benefit are venial sins. Lies told to harm someone are either mortal or venial, depending on the amount of harm they do. It is a sin to give an evasive answer when you are asked a question in school examinations or tests. In so doing, you act a lie by claiming knowledge that you do not possess.

Thus the eighth commandment of God enjoins the virtue of truthfulness. It means saying exactly what is on your mind. The word is the picture of the thought. Truth means the right picture. Truthfulness is an image of Divine Truth. God is truth, and Satan is the father of lies.[140] Jesus said, "I am the way, and the truth, and

---

[140] John 8:44.

the life."[141] He also said, "Everyone who is of the truth hears my voice."[142] As a follower of Christ, you belong to the kingdom of truth. You show your sincerity by your love for truth and your hatred of lies.

∞

Preserve the good name of others

A person commits the sin of detraction when, without a good reason, he makes known the hidden faults of another.

By the eighth commandment of God, we are commanded to speak the truth in all things, but especially in what concerns the good name and honor of others. A good name consists in the esteem with which a person is held by his fellowmen and the mutual confidence resulting from this esteem, and may refer to moral or intellectual qualities. Mutual confidence, based on mutual respect, is the foundation of all peace among people; without it, doubt, mistrust, suspicion, and ill will put in their ugly appearance.

A person's good name is his most valuable possession. The Scriptures say, "A good name is to be chosen rather than great riches."[143] Every man has a right to his good name. The right also belongs to every group — a family, a business firm, a social organization, a city, or a nation. That right remains as long as a person's faults are not public. To invade that right is to commit an injustice. Reputation is injured not only by harming the character of another but also by exaggerating another's faults. Therefore, the fact that you know another's weakness does not justify you in broadcasting that weakness. The fact that what you say is true does

[141] John 14:6.
[142] John 18:37.
[143] Prov. 22:1.

not absolve you from guilt in the matter of unjust and uncharitable talk.

Our Savior said to those who wanted to stone the woman taken in adultery: "Let him who is without sin among you be the first to throw a stone at her."[144] The saints were always most merciful; they sought in every possible way to safeguard the reputation of their fellowmen. You can do no better than follow their example.

There are circumstances in which you are justified in revealing the fault of another — for instance, in defense of yourself or another against whom an injustice has been done. The revelation, however, must be made to one who is entitled to the knowledge, because the purpose of the revelation is the correction of the fault. For example, if you come to the knowledge of a serious habit that a child in your neighborhood is guilty of, your right is to inform the parents of the child, but not the neighbors. Our Lord taught that we are to correct the erring if we are in a position to correct, and then, if that is unavailing, to speak to those who have the duty and power to correct.[145]

The damage caused by detraction can be great. According to St. Thomas, the sins against our neighbor are to be estimated "according to the damage that is done to him." Catholic theologians hold with St. Thomas that "this is a sin which by its nature is to be considered grievous." By speaking of the faults of your neighbor, you grieve him; and the dearer he holds his reputation, the more he is grieved. You lower him in the esteem of the people who know him, and you thereby undermine his honor.

As the confidence of his friends formerly gave him joy and encouraged him in his work, so now the loss of this confidence brings

---

[144] John 8:7.
[145] Cf. Matt. 18:15-17.

discouragement and depression. He begins to lose confidence even in himself and his work; he suffers a form of mental paralysis. Very frequently even his zeal in striving for virtue is weakened, for his good name was a strong incentive to prove himself worthy of it. Now he has lost that incentive.

His influence to a large extent was founded on the respect people had for him. When this respect is harmed, it is a severe blow to his activity and the good standing he needs in order to make a living and to be at peace with others. The injury is all the more harmful if the person talked about holds a position of authority. Damage may be caused that can hardly be repaired.

It may be less unkind to strike a person or to rob him of his possessions, than to lessen people's good opinion of him, for it is in the nature of man to cling to his honor far more tenaciously than to all other earthly goods.

∞

Do not even listen to detraction

Willingly to listen to detraction or to give encouragement to the detractor is to share in the sin. There would not be so many to talk about the faults of others if there were not just as many willing listeners. The speaker makes the hearer the carrier of the evil message, and the hearer encourages the speaker by listening. That explains the words of St. Bernard:[146] "It is hard to say what is worse, to injure others by words or to listen to one who does."

The peculiar nature of the sin of detraction causes many who avoid all other sins with great care to treat it carelessly and thoughtlessly. As a rule, one does not notice its effects. With other sins, such as lust, drunkenness, or theft, the result appears before

---

[146] Possibly St. Bernard (1090-1153), Abbot of Clairvaux. — ED.

our eyes, or we sense it in our soul, which opens our eyes and stirs our conscience. With uncharitable talk, everything is different; the sound of the evil word quickly dies and is soon forgotten by the speaker. He does not see how it continues to travel to numerous other people and does its mischief and harm. Besides, it sometimes parades under the guise of virtue and faithfulness to duty. St. Francis de Sales says, "He who could take away detraction from the world would take away from it a great part of its sins and iniquities."

∞

Slander ruins a person's good name through lying

A person commits the sin of slander or calumny when, by lying, he injures the good name of another. By God's command, we are obliged to esteem others and give them their due honor. St. Paul says, "Pay all of them their dues . . . respect to whom respect is due, honor to whom honor is due."[147]

Slander consists of accusing a person of faults he has never committed. The evils that follow slander are numberless. Slanderous talk is all too welcome, and it makes the rounds from mouth to mouth, ruining the reputation of its victims and sometimes causing them considerable harm even in temporal matters. Slander is a sin against justice, charity, and truth, because it violates not only the honor due to another, but also the honor that he has rightly earned by his moral character and conduct.

Slander is a verdict of guilty, pronounced in the absence of the accused, with closed doors, without defense or appeal by a disinterested and unprejudiced judge. This is the revenge of a coward. Where persons indulge in slander, there are always two who are

[147] Rom. 13:7.

actively engaged in doing wrong and one who is subjected to wrong. The one who commits slander inflicts wrong by slandering the absent; he who gives credit to the slander before he has investigated the truth is equally implicated. The innocent person is doubly injured: by him who spreads lies and by him who gives his approval to the slander.

Slander oppresses its author with the dreadful weight of his secret — the secret misery of a lie. Either he runs the risk of being cut off from society, should his lie be found out, or he has the burden of inventing many more lies to establish one lie. Most of all, slander brings eternal death — death in the eyes of God and of all good men.

To exaggerate another's faults, or to give out as certain what is uncertain or doubtful, is related to slander. The words "they say" often serve as an introduction to the most poisonous lies.

Perhaps more than anywhere else, the word of God applies here that His wrath is roused against those "who sow discord among brothers."[148] This is true, even in the most harmless case, when such talk is indulged in out of mere idle gossip. But it is far worse when unkind words have their source in hidden passions, in personal dislike, in envy, in desire for revenge, or in plain hostility.

An envious man grieves at the good name or the success enjoyed by another, and endeavors to diminish his neighbor's honor, because he is conscious of being on a lower level. A man who hates seizes every opportunity to hurt his victim in his honor, by harming him at least socially. Sometimes honor is harmed by gossip.

The continual recurrence of the same uncharitable thoughts slowly leads to blindness of judgment about one's conduct and its motives. It also happens rather frequently that, as a result of these

[148] Cf. Prov. 6:19.

harmful opinions, the speaker himself believes them to be true, despite his better knowledge. St. Gregory[149] explains this in a metaphor: "When we injure others, what else do we do but scatter dust into the air, which blinds our eyes, so that we see less of the truth, the more evil we speak about others?"

∞

Uncharitable words demand restitution

Before pardon is granted for uncharitable words, justice must be reestablished, at least in intention. The obligation to undo the harm caused by uncharitable talk does not disappear by your ignoring it. If you have taken from your neighbor, you must return. If you have damaged his property unjustly, you must make restitution. If you have sinfully harmed his good name, you are bound to repair his reputation. The greater the harm done, the more earnestly you must work at undoing it. Thus, injustice is one form of sin God does not forgive for the mere asking; He expects restitution to be made.

The worst feature of slander and detraction is that the offense can hardly ever be made good. Stolen money may be restored, but a slander is almost irrevocable. Once honor has been wounded or killed, it remains maimed or dead. What you say today in the hearing of one person travels far within a week, and you never catch up with it to revoke it. And when you make a remark in a crowd, it spreads in all directions so that it cannot be overtaken. In this respect, the one who commits the sin of slander and his victim are equally helpless.

Although you can scarcely make adequate restitution for slander or detraction, you must still make a proportionate effort. If you

---

[149] Possibly St. Gregory I (c. 540-604), Pope from 590. — ED.

have lied about another, you must let it be made known that your statements were false. If you have revealed an unknown fault, you must try to counterbalance the damage by speaking well of the person. The difficulty of making reparation ought to keep you from whatever could expose you to such a grave fall.

Joan of Arc[150] was burned at the stake in Rouen for heresy on May 30, 1431. Her story did not end with the burning; rather, it closed with a glorious ceremony of canonization on May 16, 1920. For this, credit must go to her mother, Isabel d'Arc, who pleaded before popes and kings to vindicate her daughter.

Isabel's efforts over a period of twenty years brought about the rehabilitation trial of Joan. This trial lasted six months and ended in the complete vindication of Joan.

Sins of detraction and calumny may have brought about the unjust execution of Joan. Her mother took it upon herself to repair the harm done to Joan's good name. By the trial of vindication in 1456, and the canonization of St. Joan in 1920, the Church herself has repaired the harm that had been done to Joan of Arc.

∞

Scripture condemns detraction and slander

The Old and New Testaments give us many warnings with respect to the evil of slander and detraction. In the book of Sirach, we read, "Curse the whisperer and deceiver, for he had destroyed many who were at peace. Slander has shaken many, and scattered them from nation to nation. . . . Whoever pays heed to slander will not find rest, nor will he settle down in peace. The blow of a whip raises a welt, but a blow of the tongue crushes the bones.

---

[150] St. Joan of Arc (1412-1431), French heroine who led the French army against English invaders.

Many have fallen by the edge of the sword, but not so many as have fallen because of the tongue. Happy is the man who is protected from it, who has not been exposed to its anger, who has not borne its yoke, and has not been bound with its fetters; for its yoke is a yoke of iron, and its fetters are fetters of bronze; its death is an evil death, and Hades is preferable to it."[151]

St. Peter said, "Put away all malice and all guile and insincerity and envy and all slander."[152]

And St. James deemed it necessary to give the following warning to the first believers: "Do not speak evil against one another, brethren. He that speaks evil against a brother or judges his brother speaks evil against the law and judges the law. But if you judge the law, you are not a doer of the law but a judge. There is one lawgiver and judge: He who is able to save and to destroy. But who are you that you judge your neighbor?"[153]

Since the command of Christ that we love one another as He has loved us is absolute in matters of Christian charity, it follows that the habitual destroyer of the good name of others is no friend of God, whatever his or her external pretense of piety may be. Such a person is not even a Christian by Christ's standard: "By this all men will know that you are my disciples, if you have love for one another."[154]

If you are a true follower of Christ, you will spread around you an atmosphere of sincerity that you do not allow to be troubled by the tricks of social conversation. Only where there is truth is there charity, and where charity is, there is Christianity.

---

[151] Sir. 28:13-14, 16-21.
[152] 1 Pet. 2:1.
[153] James 4:11-12.
[154] John 13:35.

∞

Do not reveal secrets without good reason

A secret is hidden knowledge that cannot be revealed without violating justice and charity. The right to secrecy is one of the most fundamental, necessary, and precious human rights.

A secret is knowledge that someone has a right to keep hidden. A person has this right because it concerns his private thoughts and actions, into which no one has a right to pry, and because secrecy is required for the protection of his life or property. Because every man has a right to his good name, no one is permitted, except for a serious reason, to dig out and reveal the secret sins of others, even though these are true.

The welfare of society also demands at times that secrecy be observed, because its violation often causes quarrels, suspicion, mistrust, and the failure of important projects. If there were no obligation to observe secrecy, those who are in need of help or advice would often have no means of assistance without the danger of bringing greater evil on themselves.

No one is allowed to try to discover the secrets of others by fraud, trickery, violence, or other unjust means. Hence it is unlawful to read letters or other private writings, to listen in on telephone conversations, to question children in order to find out intimate family matters, or to seek to gain information from others by shrewd questions.

The sin involved in the violation of secrecy may be grave or light. The gravity of the sin committed depends on the kind of secret that is involved and on the seriousness of the harm and displeasure that is caused to the owner by the breach of his secret.

A *natural secret* is so named because the duty of secrecy comes immediately from the natural law, and there need not be an agreement or promise to safeguard the secret. The natural secret obliges you under the pain of serious sin if the revelation of the knowledge would do serious injury to the character of the person who has communicated the knowledge to you. It always obliges in charity and sometimes in justice.

A *promised secret* means that, on gaining knowledge of a secret, a man promises not to reveal it. This is considered a promise of fidelity, not of justice. However, if you receive such a secret and bind yourself under a serious obligation because you consider the matter in question of great importance, you assume by that fact a serious responsibility to observe silence. It is sinful to make or keep a secret that is a violation of God's law.

An *entrusted secret* is one in which there arises the obligation of secrecy from an agreement made before the communication of the secret. In professional secrets between doctor and patient, lawyer and client, the agreement is tacit. The most sacred secret of all is that of the confessional. Under no circumstance may the seal of the confessional ever be broken.

Eavesdropping is the violation of a person's right to natural secrecy. Generally speaking, a person is guilty of a sin when he tries to overhear the conversation of others by eavesdropping, whether by hiding where he can hear the conversation or by employing some mechanical devices. Ordinarily it would be sinful for a person to listen in on the conversation of others unless he happened to be sure that nothing of importance would be said.

∞

You may violate secrecy only under certain conditions
However, there are times when the right to secrecy yields to the higher and more important rights of others — for example, when those holding the conversation are abusing the right to secrecy by plotting harm to others. To justify the use of means of

overhearing the conversation of others, you must know there is a true probability or certainty that these persons are planning something harmful and that the harm being planned is something serious, and moreover, the listening process should be conducted with the approval of lawful authority.

Certain causes excuse the violation of secrecy. There are times when you are justified in discovering, using, and revealing the secrets of others. First, you must have the consent of the person to whom the secret belongs. He may share it with as many persons as he will unless there are special reasons for not doing so. At times, you may presume the consent of the owner of the secret, when he cannot be reached in order to obtain approval and you conscientiously judge that he would give permission if asked. The more important the matter and the more likely that harm to the owner will follow, the more difficult it will be rightly to presume his consent.

Second, once something that was secret becomes public knowledge, for instance, by publication in a newspaper, your obligation of secrecy no longer exists. This holds true even though one or the other person has not read the account. However, the fact that a secret has become public knowledge does not always give you the right to use the secret. The publication of a secret in one locality does not necessarily give you the right of publishing it in other places. A man might have lost his good name in one community and later on made up for his mistake by a respectable life in another community. A person who knew him before would have no right to make known his past sin and thus destroy the reputation he has built up over the years.

Third, religious and civil superiors have a right to the knowledge necessary to fulfill their duties. When legitimately asked, those who are subject to them are bound to respond, for the right of the superior here prevails. Ordinarily superiors do not have the right to command the revelation of entrusted or professional secrets, which are generally more serious than the obligation of obedience.

Fourth, you may be excused from the obligation of secrecy when it is necessary to reveal the secret in order to prevent harm either to the common good or to the owner of the secret or to an innocent third party. St. Thomas says, "It is not lawful to receive any secret against the common good." Since the common good prevails over private advantage, you are obliged to reveal a secret when the common welfare so demands.

You are allowed to reveal a secret in order to prevent harm to the person who confided the secret to you only after you have first tried to prevail upon the person to make the matter known so that he can receive advice and help. If unsuccessful, you may make the matter known to someone who can help.

In the case of a natural or promised secret, a simple promise does not require that you maintain the secret with grave harm to yourself, nor do the laws of charity. In the case of a professional secret, you may make the truth known if the owner of the secret has deliberately thrown suspicion upon you, for you may protect yourself from unjust aggression.

In all the cases mentioned, there is present a reason that excuses from secrecy. Nevertheless, the following conditions are to be noted. First, the secret may be revealed only insofar as is necessary. Second, it may be revealed only to those who have a right to the information. Third, those to whom the secret is revealed must be placed under the obligation of entrusted secrecy not to use or reveal the secret beyond what is necessary.

Since you are conscious of your own rights in secrecy, and resentful if they are violated, be equally conscious and careful of the rights of others. For in this matter, as in all other dealings between men, the Lord's Golden Rule should be observed: "Whatever you wish that men would do to you, do so to them."[155]

⸺

Recognize the sinfulness of all forms of gossip

To gossip means to talk needlessly about the faults and failings of others and even to invent such faults and failings where none exist. To gossip means to watch closely the conduct of one's neighbor and to indulge in unwarranted criticism of his motives and in rash judgment as to the nature of his sins.

Gossip is the most common of all sins of the tongue. Although often called harmless, it is in fact rarely so because it hits at character. Character is what we are, and God knows that best. Reputation is what people say we are, and people say what they think. Your answer to what you think of a person is the reputation you give him. Reputation is the picture of character.

Revealing character means lifting up the veil and showing what is within. You reveal your character and establish your reputation by the way you speak and act. You reveal the character of another by the way you speak of and act toward him.

Gossip is drawing a *wrong* picture or drawing a picture you have no right to draw. Careless gossip is not to be tossed off lightly. God's command is "Thou shalt not bear false witness." Drawing a false picture is bearing false witness. A blow at character, if not always a mortal wound, is always a wound. A wound bleeds. Although it heals, there is always a scar left afterward.

Gossip may also give the *right* picture and still be gossip because it is drawn for those who have no right to see it. To say something that damages the reputation of another person, even if the fact

---

[155] Matt. 7:12.

stated is true, is wrong, because God gives each one a right to his reputation.

Gossip is fatal to friendship and to family happiness. We are told in the Scriptures that "a flattering mouth works ruin."[156] One of the Beatitudes in the Sermon on the Mount is "Blessed are the peacemakers, for they shall be called sons of God."[157] The opposite must also be true: "Cursed are the troublemakers, for they shall be called sons of the Devil."

Gossip, the weapon of a coward, is usually villainy born of hatred or jealousy. The scandalmonger is always busy. His stony heart and mad tongue know no pity and care not about results.

Too many people have an overgrown sense of curiosity and an uncontrollable urge to give unsolicited advice. Some busybodies pry out all sorts of neighborhood secrets and then use them as fuel for gossip, which they then carry on far and wide, often with a hypocritical pretense of charity or concern for the welfare of the community. Reputations have been blasted in this way, and serious harm done. Some of the worst examples are those who snoop their way into the homes of married people to tell them how "not to have so many children," or those who step between friends with catty, gossipy, even calumnious revelations. They become responsible for ill feelings and quarrels among friends and relatives.

It is surprising to note how many so-called good people speak uncharitably of the faults of their neighbors. These are people who are very considerate of the feelings of others when they are present, but will often say nasty things about them behind their back. These people are not wicked by nature; they are wicked solely through a desire to talk.

[156] Prov. 26:28.
[157] Matt. 5:9.

If you were to ask most people if they ever bore false witness against their neighbor, they would deny it indignantly. Yet they do bear false witness every time they discuss a piece of ill-founded gossip over coffee, on the telephone, or during visits. There is hardly anything that contributes to unhappiness and friction in a neighborhood more than thoughtless gossip.

Some of the worst sins of gossip are committed in the home. Children hear their parents using abusive language and condemning their neighbors in all sorts of ways. Neighbors' characters are hauled over the coals, their peculiarities discussed, and their weaknesses, shortcomings, and mistakes enlarged on. It is a wicked thing to teach children to become gossips and scandalmongers.

Most gossip is not serious in itself, but gossip can be a mortal sin. To spread a story, for instance, that a neighbor has been unfaithful to his wife is to damage his reputation in a serious way. If the story is false, or even if true, a grave injury has been inflicted upon him, more so than if he had been robbed of a large sum of money. If a number of people are all instrumental in spreading that false story, all of them are guilty of serious wrongdoing.

At times you may laugh at words of gossip, but it becomes very dangerous when it injures the interests of another person or damages his honor. The most harmless weakness may become a crime by reason of its consequences. Mere gossip, when it exposes another's shame, is no longer a thing to laugh about, but something that calls for your indignation.

To say that you are sorry for your own careless gossip does not forgive the sin, for that is not true contrition. Contrition is proving that you are sorry. You prove your sorrow by making up to the best of your ability for the harm you have done. If you take away a person's reputation from him, you are obliged to restore that reputation.

What is called "careless gossip" may mean detraction. If you want forgiveness for your sin of detraction, you are obliged to retract what you said. You are bound to go to every person who heard you make your remarks and take back the statement you made.

∞

Learn to avoid gossip

Following are some practical hints that may help you overcome gossip:

• *Never say behind a man's back what you are ashamed to say to his face.* Since all gossip springs from a mean and selfish human trait, it should be curbed as much as is humanly possible. Everyone has something of the busybody within him. Keep that tendency under strict control, and you will remove much unhappiness and friction in human affairs.

• *Learn to mind your own business.* You do not mind your own business if you thrust yourself into the personal affairs of others without being asked and without the motive or the means of exercising true charity; if you are a meddler who tries to interfere in other people's private transactions and human relationships; or if you are always questioning people to find out the intimate secrets of their lives. On the other hand, there is such a thing as minding your own business to excess, that is, to the exclusion of sympathy, charity, and helpfulness toward others, and to the end that you lead a selfish existence.

• *Avoid offensive curiosity.* Do not ask embarrassing personal questions, such as whether a quarrel had been patched up, or what another's financial situation is, or what wounds were caused by ungrateful friends. Do not imitate the busy-body who follows up every shred of gossip that he has over-heard, making a point to seek out persons who may know the whole story, drawing out details by pretending that he knows more than he does, and piecing together shreds of evidence that he has gotten from different persons. Do not read private letters and documents. This is an invasion of the right of privacy.

If you have a truly noble character, you will recognize where charity, sympathy, and helpfulness end, and med-dling, snooping, and interfering in the affairs of others be-gin. There is always room for true charity, for sympathy in sorrow, and for a helping hand in distress. But let your char-ity be discreet and prudent, never obnoxious, and, above all, never compromising with evil.

* *Avoid people who gossip.* If you are sensible, you will avoid the company of those who are in the habit of being bitter critics of others. Fear the evil-tongued gossip, blinded by his self-importance and pride. The gossip may give you the impression that you are a favored one to whom he con-fides his information, but when you turn your back, you may be his victim. Try to avoid letting gossips know any-thing about yourself. Never trust a gossip with your secrets.

Chapter Ten

Be charitable in your speech

Many a saint in Heaven has been sent there by a heartening word. Perhaps many a soul that is lost and shut out from God's sight forever would be a shining light in the land beyond the grave, but for the fact that someone failed to say a kind word at the proper time or failed to leave a cruel word unspoken.

The most common form of sins of anger is that of harsh, loud, intemperate words. You sin by anger in using angry words every time you raise your voice when you feel upset by something that is said or done to hurt your feelings; when you say harsh and bitter things without pausing to think of the meaning of what you are saying; when you use profanity or vulgar or even obscene words in your anger as if you are trying to shock and hurt those who cross you; when you make accusations against others that you know you have no right to make; and when you feel resentful against others.

Angry words become more harmful and more wicked when they are associated with cursing. With the tongue a person praises God, and with the tongue he curses men, who have been made after the likeness of God.[158] Cursing is a sin against the reverence

---

[158] Cf. James 3:9.

due to God's name. But another motive for avoiding it can be found in the fact that it arouses a special bitterness in the heart of its victim. No one likes to be cursed at, for cursing is an insult to one's dignity as a human being. The sensitive are deeply wounded by it.

Angry words cause smarting wounds that are hard to heal, and sometimes never heal. They are like knife stabs to the heart. Only too often, in the recklessness of anger, or in a peevish, jealous spirit, you may give vent to words you will perhaps someday regret bitterly.

A kind word is spoken as easily as a harsh one — even more easily, for with it goes the consciousness of its value and the good it will do; whereas, with the harsh, unkind word goes the consciousness of cowardice and meanness and of great harm done.

By harsh words, you write on the souls of men that which you cannot rub out. A cruel remark to your mother can write itself upon her loving heart and give her great pain. It will hurt her every time she thinks of it. To fail to give to your friend in distress a kind word may sear his soul. You cannot rub out the memory of it.

The best remedy for harsh, angry words is silence. You must learn to say nothing at all, when you know that anything said will hurt another in some way. If you are tempted to anger, train yourself to keep silence for thirty seconds and say a little prayer for patience. Then you will deal with people reasonably and effectively.

∞

Humor must never become ridicule

A harmless jest is a gift of charity to brighten and cheer a gathering. It drives away depression with a genial smile. Pleasantries occasioned by personal oddities and ludicrous circumstances are harmless in themselves. Even if they evoke laughter at one's own expense, they give life to many a get-together. They afford a desirable and often necessary safety valve.

But a jest should never be turned into a sneer. Sarcasm may originate from a talent that some have for observation of human life and its weaknesses. Certain keen-witted individuals quite readily fall into the practice of sarcastic utterance. They make it a kind of social profession to be amusing talkers, but, in doing so, they may be amusing at the expense of others. They easily wound charity by criticism, or hurt justice by revealing secrets. They have a temptation to say witty things, and, somehow, those witty things are hardly ever kind things. There is usually a drop of bitterness in them.

We all have a sharp eye for evil, which we sometimes consider a sense of humor. The habit of being sarcastic along with a talent for analyzing the character of others may be a source of much uncharitableness in life. This is a hard talent to manage, because it is so difficult to make any glory for God out of it.

Sarcasm may also have its origin in the mind that is not quite happy. When a person's own heart is not at rest, envy may urge him to hurt others. Sarcasm may also stem from ill will. Out of hatred, revengefulness, envy, or malicious joy in another's misfortune, a person may drive the sharp, poisoned dagger of sarcasm into a brother's heart in order to hurt. Ridicule adds to the misery of the world, a misery that Christ tasted during the last days of his life on earth.

Anger sometimes speaks quietly in the form of biting sarcasm. You are sarcastic when you speak in anger with scornful exaggeration of the virtues of another, such as, "Of course, you can do no wrong"; or when you express in imitation exaggerated pity for yourself, such as, "I am always the one who must give in"; or when you refer sarcastically to what other people have and what you might have if you were not tied down to your home or job, such as, "Others have something to say, but not I; I'm just a slave around here." Hardly anything puts you in the position of being disliked more completely than the sarcasm of self-pity.

Even when correction of an evil is in order, sarcasm serves no useful purpose; rather, it serves only to arouse deep resentment.

It is God's will that you respect the integrity of your fellow human beings. You are not to heap scorn on them, to belittle them, to use your tongue as a sharp tool against them.

Few things hurt more than to be laughed at when one is not trying to evoke laughter. The habit of laughing at others betrays smallness and meanness of character. You are guilty of this fault if you laugh openly at the mistakes of others as a means of manifesting how much more intelligent and wise you are: if you laugh when another mispronounces a word, or makes a mistake in grammar, or becomes confused in explaining something; or if you make use of laughter at others to express suspicion of unworthy motives or base purposes concealed beneath their words. Even if the presumption were correct (and about three out of four are not), your laughter would be mean and unkind.

The scoffer meets with his own punishment. It begins with the contempt of men. People never respect or love a person who hurts another with his jests. How can God respect such a person?

If you bruise the heart of any human being, you hurt Christ, since what is done to your neighbor is done to Him. You act like the band of criminals who once wrapped our Lord in a royal cloak and put in His hands a reed while they knelt down before Him with the mock salute: "Hail, King of the Jews!"[159] It is a terrible thing to find oneself in the company of those who mock God.

[159] Matt. 27:29.

But God is not mocked. Terrible punishment has long ago overtaken those who mocked His Son, crowned with thorns and nailed to the Cross. The ignominy of the Cross came upon the scoffing inhabitants of Jerusalem. Many of them had reason to remember how they cried, "Save Yourself! If You are the Son of God, come down from the Cross."[160]

The remedy for sarcasm in anger is humility, the smothering of your ego and honesty in appraising your blessings and crosses. A sarcastic person has a superiority complex that can be cured only by the honesty of humility.

Draw the line between innocent practical jokes and unkind, dangerous, and malicious schemes against the feelings, principles, and good nature of your friends. So-called practical jokes that interfere with another's work, or bring laughter down on his physical defects, or bring him into public scorn, are evil and unkind. If you are guilty of this type of unkindness, make a strong resolution that you will never consciously give pain to anyone.

⁓

Do not utter words of destructive criticism

Destructive criticism is one of the worst forms of uncharitableness. A destructive critic runs down, attacks, destroys, and defeats everything in theory. He is always against things or suspicious of things. He is a victim of secret pride and envy; he assails what others do because he cannot do it himself or because it may place them above him in honor.

You show signs of being a destructive critic when you are quick to throw cold water on projects and plans; when you cannot agree that any work in progress is being done properly; and when you see

[160] Matt. 27:40.

no glimmer of hope in the condition of the world. In your pessimism, you leave little room for hope and joy. If you answer to only a part of this description of a destructive critic, you will make yourself an undesirable companion even if you are not loud in expressing your views.

Belittling the accomplishments, reputations, and abilities of others is one of the more insidious forms that pride and vanity take in human characters. This vice is usually accompanied by a pretense of humility.

There is a difference between the habit of belittling others and the practice of seriously and critically discussing the merits of the work or characters of others. Objective criticism and even the expression of personal opinions about the achievements of others bring enlargement to human minds.

You are a belittler if you have the habit of thinking of belittling things to say before thinking of anything good to say about others; if you are inclined to find more fault with a certain work the more others praise it; if you think it smart to be always against things and it becomes obvious that you are not interested any longer in honest criticism, but in drawing attention to yourself.

Benjamin Franklin, tactless in his youth, became so diplomatic at handling people that he was made American Ambassador to France. The secret of his success was his policy: "I will speak ill of no man, and speak all the good I know of everybody."

Destructive criticism is *foolish*, because you have enough trouble overcoming your own limitations without fretting over the fact that God has not seen fit to distribute evenly the gift of intelligence.

Destructive criticism is *futile* because it puts a man on the defensive and usually makes him strive to justify himself. When you are tempted to criticize someone, remember that criticisms are like homing pigeons: they always return home. The person you are going to correct and condemn will probably justify himself and condemn you in return. Ninety-nine times out of a hundred, a man will not criticize himself, no matter how wrong he may be. The wrongdoer blames everybody but himself. This is human nature in action.

Nagging is a form of critical anger that expresses itself by constant complaining, ever-recurring spite and resentment, or repeated statements of grievances. Nagging is one of the infallible signs of self-pity and lack of a wholesome generosity of spirit that forgives the shortcomings of others. People who nag defend themselves on the ground that anybody would complain who had to bear the things inflicted on them by others.

You are guilty of nagging if you have one particular grievance to which you give expression in accusing language at least once every day; or if you inevitably bring up a long past sin or fault of another whenever an argument or misunderstanding arises; or if you rarely go through one full day without complaining about something you do not like. If you are inclined to nagging, you need to learn the spirit of humility, gratitude, and forgiveness.

In dealing with people, remember that you are not dealing with creatures of logic, but with creatures of emotion, bristling with prejudices and motivated by pride and vanity. Do not indulge in even a little stinging criticism, no matter how certain you are that it is justified. You will stir up a resentment that may last a lifetime.

Instead of condemning people, try to understand them. Any fool can criticize, condemn, and complain — and most fools do. But it takes character and self-control to be understanding and forgiving.

Try to figure out why people do what they do. That is a lot more profitable than criticism, and it breeds sympathy, tolerance, and kindness. You can cultivate the habit of looking first for the good points in any work or movement, and only secondly for the flaws and imperfections. You will do yourself and your friends a great service by determining to look for the good that can be found in the world and its people and now and then speak of it. Since God does not propose to judge man until the end of his days, why should you?

∞

Learn to avoid quarrels

A quarrel is a heated argument, not for the sake of enlightenment, but for self-vindication or self-defense. Petty quarreling causes much of the unhappiness in the world, and especially in the family. If you know how to avoid quarrels, you have the power of promoting happiness wherever you go.

The following suggestions will be helpful:

* *Say nothing that will arouse anger in another.* Quarreling always revolves around personalities, and its arguments are inspired by anger and pride rather than by reason. Angry quarreling serves no good purpose; it never convinces anybody of anything, and only leaves lingering bitterness.

  You lack charity in arguing with others when you substitute loudness of voice for clarity and evidence. You offend against charity when you attack others' personalities. You betray weakness of character when you meet an opponent's arguments with expressions of scorn for his ability to think, or suggestions of suspicion for his motives in holding his opinion.

  Hatred is never ended by hatred, but by love. And a misunderstanding is never ended by an argument, but by tact, conciliation, and a sympathetic desire to see the other person's viewpoint.

If you have genuine charity, you will always gladly present the truth to the erring as one of the most precious gifts of this world, but you will not seek to force it upon anyone violently. This is especially the case in trifling matters, which usually form the bone of contention in most arguments. If you should successfully settle such an unimportant quarrel, in spite of all your information and proofs, you have rendered no real service to your neighbor. All you have done is disturb and humiliate him.

Anger is responsible for protracted quarrels. If unintentionally you have said something that has aroused anger in another, withdraw from the argument at once. It takes two to quarrel, but one is enough to stop a quarrel.

• *Show respect for the other person's opinions.* It is bad judgment to try to force your opinions upon others. It would be wiser to make suggestions and let the other person think out the conclusions for himself.

If you tell him he is wrong, you will not make him want to agree with you, for you will have struck a direct blow at his intelligence, judgment, pride, and self-respect. That will make him want to strike back, but it will never make him want to change his mind. He did not ask for or want your opinion. There is no reason why you should argue with him. Most of us find ourselves changing our minds without any resistance, but if we are told we are wrong, we resent it.

The other person may be totally wrong, but he does not think so. Since there is a reason why he thinks and acts as he does, try honestly to put yourself in his place. Do not condemn him, but try to understand him. This is a sign of wisdom and tolerance.

If you are trying to see things from the other person's point of view, you will let him do a great deal of the talking. Ask him questions. If you disagree with him, you may be tempted to interrupt. But do not interrupt. He will not pay attention to you while he still has many ideas of his own crying for expression. Listen patiently and with an open mind.

Minimize your achievements. Even your friends would far rather talk to you about their achievements than listen to you boast about yours. Let your friend excel you, because that gives him a feeling of importance. You are not really too important anyway, from a worldly viewpoint. You will pass on and probably be completely forgotten a century from now.

• *If you are wrong, admit it quickly and emphatically.* Do not try to defend yourself, but admit that the other party is right. The other person will then most probably take a generous, forgiving attitude. Any fool can try to defend his mistakes — and most fools do — but it gives one a feeling of nobility to admit one's mistakes. By fighting, you never get enough, but, by yielding, you get more than you expected.

• *If you are right, try to win people gently and tactfully to your way of thinking.* People can recognize the strength or weakness of your character as well as your charity through the manner in which you discuss a disputed question with others.

It is a sign of Christian charity and of strong character to argue for a point calmly, open-mindedly, objectively, and courteously, even though warmly and earnestly. One of the most fruitful and enjoyable of human occupations is an honest, straightforward discussion. But a lack of charity and courtesy destroys all its joy and fruitfulness.

If you are going to prove anything, do it so calmly that no one will feel that you are doing it. In talking with people, do not begin by discussing the things on which you differ, but by emphasizing the things on which you agree. If a person makes a statement that you think or even know is wrong, it is better to begin by saying, "I thought otherwise, but I may be wrong. And if I am wrong, I want to be put right."

You will never get into trouble by admitting that you may be wrong. That will stop all argument and inspire the other person to be just as fair and open and broad-minded as you are. It will make him want to admit that he, too, may be wrong.

The advice Jesus gave was: "Make friends quickly with your accuser."[161] If a man's heart is filled with ill feeling toward you, you cannot win him to your way of thinking with all the logic you may use. He cannot be forced or driven to agree with you. But he may possibly be led to agree if you are gentle and friendly. If you want to win a man to your cause, first convince him that you are his sincere friend. You will then win his heart, which is the great highroad to his reason. Kindliness, the friendly approach, and appreciation can make people change their minds more readily than all the storming and harsh words you can use.

Try to practice considerateness, especially when the matter is not important and not worth disturbing anybody

[161] Matt. 5:25.

about. If it is not always possible to carry out the command of considerateness, you can do so frequently enough.

• *Be keen to perceive when somebody else's feelings are hurt.* If you find yourself in a quiet argument, and you notice that your opponent has taken something to heart by transferring the scene of action from the intellect to the feelings, that is the time to drop the argument. There are no adequate answers to hurt feelings. If you pursue your point, the argument soon grows into a quarrel.

When a person is weary, moody, or worried, he is inclined to make an issue of anything, no matter how trivial. Watch your words when you know a person is not up to par. If you can do nothing more, at least keep silence when you notice a mood that tends to make a person snap at others or even insult them.

Be prepared to have your own feelings hurt from time to time, but do not permit these hurt feelings to lead you to retaliate. A person of character swallows his vanity, suppresses his hurt feelings, and thereby avoids a quarrel.

• *Be sympathetic with another person's ideas and desires.* The man who comes to you irritated, bigoted, or unreasoning deserves very little discredit for being what he is. Sympathize with him. If you had had his environment and experiences, you would probably think and act as he does. Three-fourths of the people you will meet are hungering and thirsting for sympathy. Give it to them, and they will love you.

• *Appeal to nobler motives.* When no information can be secured about a person, the only sound basis on which to proceed is to assume that he is sincere, honest, willing, and even eager to do what is right. People generally are honest and want to discharge their obligations.

You are just as capable of making a mistake as anyone else. By insisting too eagerly upon a small right, you may turn it into a wrong against yourself and also against your neighbor. Although the letter of the law may be in your favor, its spirit may be against you.

If there is some doubt about the "right" and there are two possibilities of conceiving it, always give precedence to the certain claims of charity over your questionable right. Such consideration will not weaken the sense of justice. All that will be weakened will be the immoderate love of the things of this world that you claim as your right and for which you may so easily forget the best and holiest of rights — the right of charity.

Love is greater than the right. Remember this when there is question not of mere opinion, but of important matters — that is, when a self-opinionated person not only holds a wrong opinion, but tries to wrong you. Christ said to Peter when he tried to defend Him in the Garden of Gethsemane, "Put your sword into its sheath; shall I not drink the cup which the Father has given me?"[162] He was carrying out what He taught on another occasion: "If anyone strikes you on the right cheek, turn to him the other also."[163]

In all differences of opinion, especially in dealing with self-opinionated people, be charitable by adopting the line of conduct of Christ Himself — that is, silence. The evangelist speaks of Jesus at His trial in these words: "Jesus was silent."[164] It is not in the spirit

---

[162] John 18:11.
[163] Matt. 5:39.
[164] Matt. 26:63.

of Jesus to meet obstinacy with obstinacy when you come across an error, no matter how sure you are of your opinion.

If you follow these suggestions, you will take a sure step toward stopping an argument, eliminating ill feelings, and creating good will.

∞

Chapter Eleven

Learn to avoid speaking unkindly

If you were to make an honest resolution never to say a harsh word, you would make rapid progress on the road to holiness.

Let our Lord's words in the Gospels be your models. There was no sharpness in them. Each kind word will cost you only a moment in this world, but will have an important bearing on the kind of eternity you spend: "For by your words you will be justified, and by your words you will be condemned."[165]

Following are some remedies for unkind words:

- *Learn to be silent,* especially when you are angry or disturbed. Silence is not an end in itself, but a great means to an end — a means full of grace. Love silence as one of the great helps to avoid sin, to safeguard virtue, and to grow in close union with God. Silence is the language of God — sanctity's mother tongue.

   Remember the example of Jesus: "Jesus was silent."[166] The very expression for silence is to "hold one's peace." To break silence is to lose peace. Ask God to help you hold

165 Matt. 12:37.
166 Matt. 26:63.

your peace, especially when, by speaking, you would displease Him, offend another, or disturb your own peace of soul. Be an instrument of His peace wherever you are placed in the world. Silence will be your strongest aid.

Some people cannot bear to keep a secret, because they never learned the noble art of keeping silence. They cannot rest until they have given away, at first only in bits, but in the end entirely, any confidential information brought to their knowledge. Do not track down your neighbor's faults. Should you happen to come to the knowledge of your neighbor's hidden fault, let charity seal the knowledge in your heart as in a deep grave. Never open this grave before the eyes of man without a very serious reason. When you are tempted to speak about another's secret faults, ask yourself, "Why should I do this?"

St. Margaret Mary says, "Above all, let us carefully keep silence on occasions that mortify us. Let us be charitable and humble, both in our thoughts and words."

• *Don't repeat gossip and slander.* If laziness is rightly called "the beginning of all vice," that is particularly true of the sins of the tongue. As long as you do your work with full interest, you will have neither the time nor the inclination to take part in unkind talk.

Talk is cheap, but, like other cheap things, it is apt to become expensive in the end. Silence is golden; talk is brazen. The busiest thing on earth is an idle rumor. The idle tongue works, not merely all day, but overtime every day. A good rule to follow is: "Mind your own business."

Carefully sift the talk you hear. Speak your mind, if you will, but mind what you speak. The talebearer is as bad as a talemaker, if not worse. The man who says a mean thing about another is not so mean as the man who repeats it.

Bear in mind the admonition of St. John Chrysostom:[167] "Let us flee. my beloved, let us flee the slanderous talks, since we know that this vice is an abyss in which the Devil reigns and plots his most sinister plans."

The religion of the man who does not govern his tongue is vain. God gave you one mouth and two ears. This indicates the ratio of two to one, which should prevail between speaking and listening. A perfectly adjusted tongue always runs slower than the mind. A person who repeats half of what he hears talks too much. Make this your watchword: "In private, watch your thoughts; in the family, your temper; and in company, your tongue." St. James says, "If anyone makes no mistakes in what he says, he is a perfect man."[168]

Never speak of even the lesser sins and faults of others. When circumstances arise where it is permissible to speak of them, make your remarks with moderation, and exclude bitterness and hatred. It is virtuous to respect the absent, for they have no opportunity for explanation or self-defense.

• *Openly oppose uncharitable talk, or counteract it by eloquent silence*. Most people would not talk so easily about the faults of others if they were not certain that their listeners like to hear what they are saying. The speaker makes the hearer the carrier of the evil messages, and the hearer encourages the speaker by listening. That explains the words of St. Bernard: "It is hard to say what is worse, to injure others or to listen to one who does."

[167] St. John Chrysostom (c. 347-407), Bishop of Constantinople.
[168] James 3:2.

If you see that you would accomplish nothing by openly defending the person talked about, then keep silence. It is a great work of charity to indicate by your conduct that uncharitable talk disgusts you quite as much as impure stories do. So don't excuse yourself with the question: "Can I help it when people talk?" Yes, indeed you can — when they talk to *you*. Although you may complain about evil gossip and slander, will you leave in the middle of a slanderous tale, or at least show no interest in it? The really effective way to stop a wagging tongue is to stop your ears.

• *Speak of things, not of people.* Everyone has a right to a good name. Yet what frail guards are posted around the good reputation of each of us! One slip of the tongue may do lifelong damage. Even the most bitter repentance cannot repair the damage once it is done. If you cannot say anything good about someone, say nothing at all.

When you are speaking evil of a woman, picture your own mother or sister in her place. When you are speaking evil of a man, picture your own father or brother in his place. Even when you think you are right, you may be wrong; therefore, distrust hearsay. It is just as cowardly to judge an absent person as it is wicked to strike a defenseless one. Only the ignorant and narrow-minded gossip, for they speak of persons instead of things.

• *Don't deceive yourself by false excuses for unkind talk.* Do not say, "What I said wasn't so bad or important." Too often, unkind words have their source in hidden passions, personal dislike, envy, desire for revenge, or plain hostility. You must weigh the damage done, which may be great even in what you consider a trifling matter.

Don't try to quiet your own misgivings by saying, "What I said was true." That makes the sin one of detraction rather than one of slander, but it remains a sin, and the damage done may be exactly the same in both cases. Even if the fault of another is true and known, gossiping about it serves no useful purpose. To offer a charitable word of mercy, of excuse, or of forgiveness is the Christlike approach.

Don't say, "I told the person to keep it confidential." If someone else is not allowed to reveal the secret, why did you? How can you expect others to be silent when you yourself were careless?

Regarding this, St. John Chrysostom remarks: "This is ridiculous: they tell me something as a secret, begging and beseeching that the secret be kept. By this, they plainly indicate that they themselves have done something very reproachable, for if the other is not allowed to divulge the secret, why should you? How can you expect others to be silent and careful when you were not so yourself?"

• *Avoid harsh words.* Harsh words wound the heart and disturb the soul. Don't be guilty of unkindness in a spirit of bravado by trying to coax forth the laughter of others at the expense of a fellowman. Such wisecracking never pays. It hurts, arouses resentment, and engenders hate. Detest personal remarks and biting sarcasm. A remark that hurts has ceased to be a joke. If you want to keep those you love close to you, laugh *with* them, not *at* them.

Thoughtless, catty remarks about others have probably created more unnecessary enemies than any other form of human behavior. Take particular pains to see that your tongue is used for good, never for evil: to console, not to condemn; to build up, not to tear down; to rejoice at the good fortune of others, not to begrudge their success.

• *Bear with your neighbor in spite of his faults.* You yourself have faults others must bear with. Besides, how easily you exaggerate the faults of others, especially of those toward whom you feel a natural dislike! Rather, overlook their faults, and ask yourself if it is fair to notice the speck of dust in your neighbor's eye when perhaps there is a log in yours.[169] This kind attitude will teach you how to appreciate the good in others and to speak kindly of them.

St. Margaret Mary's sound advice is this: "Be humble toward God and gentle with your neighbor. Judge and accuse no one but yourself, and ever excuse others. Speak of God always to praise and glorify Him; speak of your neighbor only with respect. Do not speak of yourself at all, either well or ill."

• *Remember the punishment for unkind talk.* Uncharitable talk should cause you deep concern. You need only think of God's judgment and the account that you will have to render on the observance of the eighth commandment. Remember our Lord's warning: "On the Day of Judgment, men will render account for every careless word they utter."[170]

If you thoughtlessly allow your tongue to wag or make it the tool of anger or hatred; if you let yourself be swayed by bad temper, selfishness, and vanity; or if you judge and blame rashly, you will gather before God a mountain of evil, the height of which will not be known to you until you

[169] Cf. Matt. 7:3.
[170] Matt. 12:36.

realize the true meaning of Christ's words: "As you did it to one of the least of these my brethren, you did it to me."[171]

Begin today to see how you stand on this point, and be determined to improve. Tomorrow may be too late. As St. Augustine tells us, God has promised forgiveness to your repentance, but He has not promised tomorrow to your procrastination.

• *Imitate the graciousness of Christ.* Graciousness is the quality of being sincerely kind and loving toward others in word and deed, of bestowing favors courteously, and of rendering services freely and affably. Cordiality and graciousness of manner attract your fellowmen most powerfully to the practice of virtue. By His graciousness, Christ won many, such as Mary Magdalene, away from evil and led others, such as His own Mother, to greater sanctity. He said, "Take my yoke upon you, and learn of me, because I am meek and humble of heart; and you shall find rest to your souls."[172]

St. Margaret Mary describes the reaction of the Sacred Heart to unkindness in these words: "He wishes you to conform your heart to the virtues of His own. If you only knew how much you grieve Him when you fail in charity and humility, or when, through cowardice, you neglect to use the lights He gives you to make you withdraw from worldliness."

St. Paul advises, "Conduct yourselves wisely toward outsiders, making the most of the time. Let your speech always be gracious, seasoned with salt, so that you may know how

[171] Matt. 25:40.
[172] Matt. 11:29 (Douay-Rheims edition).

you ought to answer everyone."[173] The salt of wisdom ought to flavor your conversation at all times. Wisdom is shown by being silent or saying the right thing at the right time. If you are supernaturally kind and wise, the Holy Spirit will help you to give the appropriate answers to questions addressed to you.

• *Pray for your neighbor.* If you pray for unsympathetic persons half as much as you talk about their faults, how many sins would you avoid and how much happier your life would be! Into a prayerful soul the poisonous vapors of sin cannot enter, because such a soul is filled by God and His grace. Wherever God is, there is light and love and peace.

Pray for yourself also, that God may help you to become supernaturally gracious toward others — to add an encouraging smile to the word you may speak, a heartening tone to your often-colorless voice, and a gentleness of touch in the act that otherwise might be too rigorous.

[173] Col. 4:5-6.

∞

Chapter Twelve

Use kindness in correcting others

Correction, or reproof, is the act of authoritatively blaming another openly and directly for wrong. It is a direct expression of disapproval to the person reproved and is evidently a duty of those who stand in governing positions over others, such as ecclesiastical authorities, representatives of the law, parents, employers, teachers — in fact, those who must protect the true interests of the professions generally.

When gentle exhortation and encouragements fail, charity must use the road of correction. But a correction should be an expression of love. Christ did not hesitate to utter words of reproof. He rebuked Capernaum and Jerusalem, the Apostles, and even Peter. God rebukes every wrong through the voice of conscience.

Only warranted correction is lawful. Reproof is warranted when there is question of sin and those lesser faults that easily lead to sin. Our Lord said, "Take heed to yourselves; if your brother sins, rebuke him, and if he repents, forgive him; and if he sins against you seven times in the day, and turns to you seven times and says, 'I repent,' you must forgive him."[174] Not mere personal

---

[174] Luke 17:3-4.

restitution to the offended one is referred to, but the correction and salvation of the erring one, for Christ said, "If he listens to you, you have gained your brother."[175]

A person's character seems to be fully revealed in the exercise of his authority. You cannot help revealing greatness or smallness, selfishness or considerateness, by the way you treat those who are made subject to you — whether you are a parent in a home, a manager in an office, a rich man in society, or a superior or officer in an organization.

A sign of weakness of character is to exercise your authority in a spirit of self-exaltation by being pompous, frequently referring to your authority and insisting beyond all reason on deference.

It is a sign of weakness of your character if you give the impression that failure to perform a duty — or sometimes even an unconscious mistake — on the part of someone who is subject to you is really a personal insult. If you are great-souled, you will forget yourself when you have to correct and you will consider only the success of the work to be done and the good of the one to be corrected.

You also show weakness of character when you speak or act as if authority brought with it perfect knowledge, prudence, judgment, and ability in all things.

If you are strong of character, you will always be simple and unassuming, no matter what authority you bear, because you will realize that authority is a necessary means of unity among men for the accomplishment of some great good. To be strong of character means that you will recognize your weaknesses no matter how much authority you possess. You will consult others and heed advice; you will ask for help and freely delegate your power.

[175] Matt. 18:15.

∞

Correct motives must govern your admonition

To admonish successfully, you need delicacy of feeling and great tactfulness. If you wish to attain proper results through your admonition, you must be governed by correct motives. These motives are:

- *Zeal for the observance of God's law:* you should withhold a reproof if circumstances seem to indicate that the desired good will not be effected. Such a reproof may make matters worse, for the reproved will be prompted to do greater mischief and become more incorrigible. Or perhaps another person would be able to give the reproof more successfully.

- *The correction of the offender:* you have done a beautiful work of mercy and shown noble charity if you have turned a fellow Christian away from evil ways.

- *Responsibility in the matter:* you will be charged with neglect of duty if you fail to aid an erring neighbor when it was in your power to have done so.

∞

Be slow to correct

If charity demands it, do not be afraid to speak words of correction, but do not be hasty in doing so. First deliberate whether it is worthwhile, for some people like to correct others for mere trifles. St. Paul says to Timothy, "Convince, rebuke, and exhort, be unfailing in patience and in teaching."[176] The result of a hasty correction is that it loses its power or produces a contrary effect.

[176] 2 Tim. 4:2.

Then consider whether a correction alone will lead to your neighbor's amendment. Do not let your correction be a result of mental sloth which will not take the trouble to look for other means to correct your neighbor. A correction may seem like a short cut, but it is not always the most prudent and certain way. First pray for guidance before you speak. Be eager to praise, slow to rebuke: in this consists true nobility of soul.

∞

Correct others out of love

Let your correction spring from love, never from irritation. People often rebuke others not because of a wrong done but because of annoyance. They are not always unhappy because of the faults they blame, but they are at least unconsciously pleased to have someone on which to vent their temper.

Never correct out of sheer harshness or pride. It cannot be right to remind others continually of their shortcomings simply because you are virtuous. "You are inconsiderate" is often meant to convey, "I am always considerate." Unless a correction springs from charity, it cannot be justified before God.

Never let correction degenerate into injuries or insults, nor let there be anything about it that could hurt or give offense. Abuse does not correct or even humble; rather, it rouses a person to a secret and more bitter hatred. When people meet abuse with abuse, they make an exhibition entirely unworthy of human beings.

A correction that springs from a loving heart and is administered in a kindly way will lead to good results. The music of love, whether it is heard in the soft tones of praise or the sterner notes of correction, never fails to call for a return of love.

St. Paul says that correction ought to be given in a truly brotherly way. "Brethren, if a man is overtaken in any trespass, you who are spiritual should restore him in a spirit of gentleness. Look to yourself, lest you, too, be tempted."[177]

Be understanding enough to appreciate the type of reaction that in all probability will rise up in the person being reproved, and be able to cope with it. Reproof is hard for human nature to take. A cutting humiliation in most cases, it may often cause bitter resentment and sharp anger, or it may arouse contempt and consequent disregard. In either case, the desired good will be frustrated.

If you are motivated by true love of God and of neighbor, your reproof will be given gently. A tenderness characteristic of holiness will be felt by the one receiving the reproof. Nothing attracts the heart of man so strongly as manifestations of love. St. Paul counsels "restoring" the one gone astray, not judging or chastising. He says, "You who are spiritual should restore him in a spirit of gentleness." St. Paul urges us to "warn him like a brother." He says: "Brethren, do not be weary in well-doing. If anyone refuses to obey what we say in this letter, note that man, and have nothing to do with him, that he may be ashamed. Do not look on him as an enemy, but warn him as a brother."[178]

The best results will be attained in admonishing another if you touch the sensitive nature of the reproved with a tenderness like that of Christ. Make commendations of the good qualities in the person freely and generously, not in the spirit of flattery, but as a testimony of certain existing excellences which might be made more far-reaching in results, if other hindrances were not present. Speak briefly but definitely regarding the objectionable point. Much teaching and sermonizing are ineffectual. The reproved will recognize quickly enough all that is intended.

[177] Gal. 6:1.
[178] 2 Thess. 3:13-15.

Let the reproved realize that you are merely making recommendations for his true welfare and possible greater influence, and that you are submitting advice to him to use at his own discretion.

If the tables were turned, and you were the one being justly reproved, you know well enough that you would want to be dealt with considerately. You need the guidance of the Holy Spirit in this very delicate work of charity.

Thus St. Paul says: "Bear one another's burdens, and so fulfill the law of Christ. For if anyone thinks he is something, when he is nothing, he deceives himself. But let each one test his own work, and then his reason to boast will be in himself alone and not in his neighbor. For each man will have to bear his own load."[179]

- *Begin with praise.* If you must find fault, begin with praise and honest appreciation. It is always easier to listen to unpleasant things after you have heard some praise of your good points. Do not use the hammer-and-dynamite method. Call attention to people's mistakes indirectly.

- *Talk about your own mistakes before criticizing others.* It isn't nearly so difficult to listen to the recital of your own faults if the criticizer begins by humbly admitting that he, too, is far from being without fault.

- *Ask questions instead of giving direct orders.* This makes it easy for a person to correct his error, and it saves a man's pride and gives him a feeling of importance. It makes him want to cooperate instead of rebel.

- *Protect the good name of people.* We often ride roughshod over the feelings of others, getting our own way, finding

[179] Gal. 6:2-5.

fault, issuing threats, or criticizing a child or an adult in front of others, without even considering the hurt to the person's pride. A few minutes' thought, a considerate word or two, and a genuine understanding of the other person's attitude would go far toward alleviating the sting.

• *Praise every slightest improvement.* Praise, not condemnation, inspires the other person to keep on improving.

• *Give a person a fine reputation to live up to,* and he will make great efforts rather than see you disillusioned. If you want to improve a person in a certain respect, act as though that particular trait were already one of his characteristics. Assume and state that the other person has the virtue you want him to develop. Almost everyone, rich or poor, lives up to the reputation of honesty that is bestowed upon him.

• *Use encouragement.* Make the fault that you want to correct seem easy to correct; make the thing you want the other person to do seem easy to do.

Tell a child, a husband, or friend that he is stupid at a job and that he is doing it all wrong, and you will have destroyed almost every incentive to improvement. But if you are liberal with your encouragement and make the thing seem easy to do, and let the other person know that you have faith in his ability to do it, he will strive hard to excel.

∞

Receive correction graciously
When you receive correction, follow these guidelines:

• *Listen without interrupting* until the person reproving you has had his say. This self-renunciation will give you poise of spirit, and offer you an opportunity to invoke the Holy Spirit for help as to how to conduct yourself.

* *Offer to consider the matter.* If the charge is unfair or false, have at least the courage and good will to say that you will take time to study yourself in the matter, although you cannot see the case as presented.

* *Refrain from violent backfire or haughtiness* in speech or act, especially in cases where the charge is false. Self-defense or expressed indignation at injustice easily gives others the opportunity to surmise consciousness of guilt, at least in some degree, on your part. On the other hand, the acceptance of an unjust reproof graciously and cheerfully is generally admitted as one sign of innocence regarding the imputed evil.

* *Try to cultivate the feeling of gratitude to* God for the occasion to suffer for His sake. Make the reproof an opportunity to practice love of enemies and to test the quality of your love of God. Ask Christ for the grace to be silent as He was when basely subjected to the contempt of His judges and of the people on that first Good Friday.

Chapter Thirteen

Seek the blessings of kind words

There is hardly anything in the world that costs less and is worth more than a kind word. Many things are done by men, and at far greater cost, that yet do not confer on the world half the blessings that flow from one single word of love.

Kind words are a creative force, a power that concurs in the building up of all that is good, an energy that showers blessings upon the world. They are a blessing upon both the speaker and the hearer. The inspired writer in the Scriptures cries out, "A word in season, how good it is!"[180]

∞

Kind words have an irresistible power

Love is its own reward in that it yields interior joy, peace, strength, and freedom. But it is also rewarded by men. People are likely to help one who loves them rather than one who shows them dislike or indifference.

Man can do without many things, but not without man. If we want to create and achieve great things in this world, we must try

---

[180] Prov. 15:23.

to secure the cooperation of men. Love alone gives power, a royal power to rule and to guide, aroused only by having charity and showing it. There is no substitute for charity.

Not only the help but above all the love of our fellowmen is necessary. Man is like a plant that needs the warm sunshine of human and loving companionship all during life. There is hardly a power on earth equal to the power of kind words. That power seems to be beyond natural causes. There is no one — no matter how wicked, pessimistic, or disgusted with life he may be — who will not respond to kindness and sympathy.

∞

Kind words have the power
to destroy prejudices

Suppose for a long time you have had prejudices against a person that seemed extremely well founded. Some particular circumstances bring you into contact with this person. Kind words pass, and the prejudices thaw away, for you now honestly see nothing in the person that would warrant your prejudices. The power of the simple kind word has changed everything.

You may have regarded another with distrust, so much so that you were not likely to be friends with that person; you and the other person may have been set against each other by the circulation of gossip; or you and the other may have been looked upon as rivals. But a kind word — or perhaps the mere report of a kind word — has been enough to set all things straight and begin an enduring friendship.

Others may betray hatred toward you only because they expect unkindness. When they receive instead a kind word or gesture, they are defenseless and they often return the kindness they are given.

∞

Kind words put an end to quarrels

Even one-sided quarrels, which are the hardest to set right, give way in time to kind words. Most quarrels result from a misunderstanding. Many live by silence, which only increases the misunderstanding. Renewed explanations become new misunderstandings. Kind words, patiently uttered, are your only hope. They will not explain what has been misunderstood, but they will do what is much better: they will make explanation unnecessary, and so avoid the risk of reopening old wounds.

Other words all too frequently create enmities and further embitter existing misunderstandings, but one simple word of love is enough at times to bring about a reconciliation. One such word may be enough to remove an aversion for which there may not have been a reason, or to dispel a misunderstanding.

Little phrases such as "I am proud of you," "What is your opinion?" "If you please," and "Thank you" are courtesies that oil the cogs of the monotonous grind of everyday life. They are the hallmark of good breeding.

Begin by applying this magic touchstone of appreciation right at home. There is no other place where it is more needed — or more neglected. Your family must have some good points. How long has it been since you expressed your admiration for any of them?

∞

Kind words soothe and comfort

Our Lord never met a sad person for whom He did not have a word of comfort, a fearful person for whom He did not have a word of encouragement, a persecuted person whom He did not defend, or a needy person whose request He refused to grant. To the widow

191

of Nain, after having sympathized with her loss, He said, "Do not weep,"[181] and then raised her only son to life. Even on the Cross, He spoke to a criminal wonderful words of love: "Truly, I say to you, today you will be with me in Paradise."[182]

Sometimes things pile up and the heart becomes heavy with frustration or doubts, and we feel unable to cope with the pressures of daily living. At such times, you long for someone to whom you can pour out the dark thoughts afflicting you — someone who will sympathize with you in your trouble. Even if that person can offer no solution, his careful attention to what you have to say begins to ease your tension and to lighten your load of depression.

Talk in which you feel free to unburden your heart is a most effective tranquilizer — it not only soothes; it encourages. It injects new confidence. Things start looking up.

When there is a question of comforting, congratulating, or defending another, long and well-chosen words are not necessary. Our Lord's words of comfort, recognition, and blessing were ever perfectly simple and natural. True love nearly always finds spontaneously the most appropriate words. The more specific your praise, the more deeply it will be apt to touch its recipient. But praise should be spontaneous. You do not have to look for opportunities to say complimentary things. Such opportunities will come unbidden. The important thing is that you do not neglect these opportunities, but utilize them by uttering words that will brighten other lives.

Do not use flattery. The difference between appreciation and flattery is this: one is sincere and the other insincere; one is unselfish and the other selfish; one is universally admired and the other

[181] Luke 7:13.
[182] Luke 23:43.

is universally condemned. Flattery seldom works with discerning people.

When you are not engaged in thinking about some definite problem, you usually spend about ninety-five percent of your time thinking about yourself. Stop thinking of your accomplishments, your wants. If you stop thinking about yourself for a while and begin to think of another person's good points, you will not have to resort to cheap and false flattery that can be spotted at once.

Give honest, sincere appreciation. Be hearty in your approbation and lavish in your praise, and people will cherish your words and repeat them even after you have forgotten them. Charity somehow imparts dignity and depth to the simplest speech, for charity really is the wisest and deepest thing in the world. Good will is all that is required to make the simplest words eloquent.

Daily you come across anxious, excited, sad, and fearful people to whom you might speak a kind word. How often a person is humbled or made the object of attack in your presence, yet you remain silent. Among those around you, there may be one who, for a long time, has deserved a word of recognition, yet you forget to utter it. How often you might offer good wishes to a friend or acquaintance, but you are too cold or reserved to speak that gracious word.

Do not let your indolence, reserve, or selfishness keep you from opening your mouth. Selfishness may show itself when your personal profit or advantage is at stake, or when you have a certain aversion for your neighbor or a lingering ill feeling against him.

∞

Kind words encourage

To praise your neighbor is an act of charity that brings joy. God Himself so fashioned the human heart that it needs praise, for the same reason that it dreads contempt. Even those who do not perform their good works for the sake of being praised are gladdened by praise, because it means that their good will, their efforts, and their achievements are known and recognized.

Nobody is so completely and constantly self-assured that he never requires a word of praise, a pat on the back, or a kind suggestion. Just to be told sincerely that you are doing a good job encourages you to do even better. The slightest recognition can have a tonic effect. Probably the deepest urge in human nature is the desire to be important. Everybody likes a compliment. Everybody likes to be appreciated. This craving makes people do the most difficult things.

The average man complains if he doesn't like something; if he does like it, he says nothing. We nourish the bodies of our children and friends. But how often do we nourish their self-esteem by giving them the hearty appreciation that they crave?

Praise is meant to be a constructive force in the kingdom of God on earth. It directs many a soul toward everlasting bliss and apostolic zeal. Praise encourages; silence discourages. Many have remained stationary in striving for holiness or have even fallen back because no one thought it worthwhile to bestow the recognition of praise upon their first effort and their success.

Praise may make a person vain and slothful if he happens to be a shallow character. When you praise another, always point out some such objective, lest the person praised should lazily rest on his laurels.

St. Paul did not hold the attitude of certain people who never praise anyone. He said, "I commend you because you remember me in everything and maintain the traditions even as I have delivered them to you."[183] To be stingy with your praise is a defect that

[183] 1 Cor. 11:2.

194

may be the result of a kind of laziness. You take no interest in the progress and victories of your neighbors; you do not rejoice with those who rejoice. A kind of horrible jealousy may keep you from speaking up to give credit where credit is due. Or a lack of knowledge of the human heart, which makes you imagine that your neighbor does his duty without effort or difficulty, so that he needs no encouragement, may hold back your praise.

By such indifference, you deprive yourself of the pleasure of giving to another the reward of his labor. What if God also were to remain silent in the hour when you hope to hear from His lips the blessed praise: "Well done, good and faithful servant . . . enter into the joy of your Master"?[184]

You will not know what precise effect your praise has. You utter it and go on your way, leaving it to work its magic. A wife's words of encouragement may give her husband renewed strength to tackle a difficult task in connection with his work, yet she may never know that it was her words that had such a profound effect. A teacher's encouraging remarks may be instrumental in persuading a child to choose a particular career, but it is unlikely that the teacher will ever know it.

Encouragement is something silent rather than spoken. Just by being present at an activity, you encourage those who are responsible for its success. For instance, if you are a member of an organization that meets regularly, you encourage the officers of that organization by your attendance at meetings.

When you bestow praise, be sure to pay tribute to the help of God. Thus, in praising Peter, our Lord also addressed a word of praise to God: "Blessed are you, Simon Bar-Jona! For flesh and blood has not revealed this to you, but my Father who is in

[184] Matt. 25:21.

Heaven."[185] He directed the gaze of His apostle not only upward but forward to that which lay before Him — the heavy task He was yet to accomplish: "And I tell you, you are Peter, and on this rock I will build my Church, and the powers of death shall not prevail against it."[186]

Inspire the people with whom you come in contact to a realization of the hidden treasures they possess, and you can transform those people. The reason is that usually people make use of only a small part of their physical and mental resources.

∽

Kind words bring happiness

The double reward of kind words is the happiness they cause in you and in others. When a kind word proceeds from your lips, it blesses you first. Uttering kind words is a happiness in itself. In your everyday life, you are at times confronted by problems and weighed down by trials. Your heart is gripped by worry and sorrow. Life becomes almost unbearable. Yet, if you still greet others with kind words and a cheerful disposition, the effect will be to put your own worries to flight and to lift up your spirits. A kind word fills you with the gladness that gain or pleasure can never procure. A moment when God is so near as almost to be felt is nearly always the reward of a kind word.

Happiness follows close upon kind words. They soothe your own irritation and charm your cares away. They draw you near to God and spread abroad the peace of God within your heart. They produce in you a sense of quiet restfulness, like that which accompanies the consciousness of forgiven sin.

[185] Matt. 16:17.
[186] Matt. 16:18.

Even the body is included in the blessings of a kind word, for your face will show those gentle, kindly lines that will make others think of the very person of our Lord Himself. Even outwardly a Christian may become like Him who is the incarnate Word of love.

Kind words make others happy. How often have you yourself been made happy by kind words, in a manner and to an extent that you cannot explain? No analysis enables you to detect the secret of the power of kind words. Even self-love is found inadequate as a cause.

Of all the gifts of nature to man, the one that brings the most rejoicing is sunshine. So, too, are sunny human beings. The most blessed of gifts is kindly affection. Like the sun, it will bring forth flowers of kindness. A few kind words or a little forbearance will often raise the shutters in your house, darkened by the clouds of discord and unhappiness, to let in a flood of sunshine.

∞

Words have a power of their own for good

If you are kind-worded, you are a genial person, and geniality is power. Nothing sets wrong right so soon as geniality. No reformation succeeds unless it is genial. No one was ever corrected by sarcasm — rushed, perhaps, but never drawn nearer to God. The genial man is the only successful man. Nothing can be done for God without geniality. More plans fail for the want of kindness than for the want of anything else.

Kind words may be more influential than even actions. Kind words prepare man for conversion. Like angels of grace, they are the saving messengers of divine mercy. They procure entrance for wholesome counsels into their souls. Kind words have converted more sinners than zeal, eloquence, or learning. There never was a more effective means to guide men into the path of conversion, sanctification, and eternal salvation than words inspired by love. By their power of producing happiness, they have also a power of producing holiness, and so of winning men to God.

Kind words win for you many graces from God — especially the spirit of contrition. Everything that makes you gentle has at the same time a tendency to make you contrite.

Kind words make you truthful, because what is untruthful is not kind. Kind words make you truthful, since kindness is God's view, and His view is always the true view. Insincerity is a heavy burden of which kind words relieve you.

The more humble you are, the more kindly you will speak. The more kindly you speak, the more humble you will grow. An air of superiority is foreign to genuine kindness.

Kind listening, as well as kind speaking, is also a grace. Just listening to other people is a superbly effective way of encouraging them, and that is a great act of charity. This requires a willingness to be silent, to let the other person tell his own story in his own way. You will realize that the other person is suffering spiritual pain and that you can alleviate that pain only by listening quietly and compassionately. Such listening becomes an exquisite expression of love.

Kind listening is often an act of the most delicate interior self-denial and is a great help toward kind speaking. If you govern others, you must take care to be a kind listener, lest you offend God and fall into secret sins. Repress vexation when you meet people with peculiar characters who make a specialty of irritating you. They always come at the wrong time and say the wrong things. A person may run to you with an imaginary sorrow when you are bearing a real one. Or he may address you with a loud voice and boisterous laugh when your nerves are on edge. Or he may pour out the exuberance of his happiness when you are worried or fearful. All this is excellent material for self-sanctification.

Be a good listener. Encourage others to talk about themselves. Exclusive attention to the person who is speaking to you is very important; nothing else is so flattering.

Become genuinely interested in people. Remember that the person you are talking to is a hundred times more interested in himself and his wants and his problem than he is in you and your problems. You can make more friends in two weeks by becoming interested in other people than you can in two months by trying to get other people interested in you. Talk in terms of the other person's interests. The royal road to a man's heart is to talk to him about the things he treasures most. The individual who is not interested in his fellowman has the greatest difficulties in life and causes the greatest harm to others.

Therefore, ask questions that the other person will enjoy answering. Encourage him to talk about himself and his accomplishments, and you will not only be a good conversationalist, but a friend.

Kind words cost you nothing, yet how often do you fail to use them. Although opportunities are frequent, you sometimes show no eagerness to embrace them. On the occasions when they imply some degree of self-sacrifice, they almost instantly repay you a hundredfold.

Try to form the habit of saying kind words. With the help of God's grace you can do so. When once this habit is formed, it is not quickly lost. The more you know yourself, and the more you are united to God, the more soul-gratifying you will find the practice of saying kind things. Although you are weak and needy, make up your mind to do some good in this world while you are in it. Kind words are the chief implements you can use for this work.

Part Three

∞

Show your love in kind deeds

Chapter Fourteen

Chapter Fourteen

∞

Guard against giving bad example

The love of neighbor forbids certain sins that would bring unhappiness or spiritual or temporal harm on him. Spiritual harm includes such things as scandal and cooperation in another's sin.

Scandal is to be found in any word or deed or even omission that is evil in itself, or has the appearance of evil, and that can be the occasion of spiritual damage to another. For example, a mother and father who carelessly miss Mass on Sunday are giving scandal to their children by helping them to look without fear on the mortal sin of missing Sunday Mass.

∞

Direct scandal leads others
deliberately into sin

Direct scandal is committed by a person who deliberately tries to induce another to commit sin. Whenever a person urges, advises, coaxes, or commands another person to commit a mortal sin, he is guilty of the mortal sin of direct scandal, whether he succeeds in his intent or not.

The following would be guilty of grave and direct scandal: a wife urging her husband to practice contraception (or vice versa);

relatives or friends of a validly married but divorced Catholic urging him or her to keep steady company with someone and even attempt remarriage; one who sells, lends, or gives away lewd books, obscene pamphlets, or impure pictures that by their very nature offer strong inducements to bad thoughts, desires, and actions in those who read or see them; women who deliberately appear in public in so immodest a way that they know they will attract lustful glances and desires of men who see them; one who argues with others against the truths of religion, or speaks of them disparagingly or contemptuously, or criticizes and condemns priests and bishops so bitterly that others are bound to be strongly tempted to become disobedient to lawful authority; and a husband who ridicules and places obstacles to his wife's attempts to live up to the important duties of her religion.

∞

Bad example is a form of scandal

Indirect scandal is that in which the sinner does not directly intend or urge another to commit a sin, but knows that his words or actions or omissions may easily have that effect.

Most forms of indirect scandal come under the heading of bad example that one knows may have a damaging spiritual effect on others. Bad example can become serious scandal. The bad example of anyone who holds authority over others always has an especially evil effect, such as the bad example of slandering others seriously or cursing in the presence of children.

One person drinking to excess can draw others along with him into the same sin. One person telling an obscene story can be responsible for many such stories being told. One person starting a conversation about the secret serious sins of an absent person can draw out all sorts of defamatory stories from others.

∞

Scandal is an enemy of charity

The worst sin against brotherly love is scandal, because it contributes to the most terrible tragedy that can befall a human being, namely, the loss of his immortal soul. It is contrary to charity to inflict unnecessary pain on a fellow human being even here in this world.

Our Lord forcefully condemns those who are guilty of this sin. "Whoever causes one of these little ones who believe in me to sin, it would be better for him to have a great millstone fastened round his neck and to be drowned in the depths of the sea. Woe to the world for temptations to sin! For it is necessary that temptations come, but woe to the man by whom temptation comes!"[187]

Giving scandal may be a mortal or a venial sin, according to the degree of spiritual damage one's words, actions, or omissions may cause in others. To draw others into unkind but not serious gossip about the absent is the venial sin of scandal. To encourage or urge, or by example to lead others into any mortal sin, would itself be the mortal sin of scandal.

Scandal adds to the evil of the actions or words or omissions the new guilt of assisting others to defile their souls and to offend God. Therefore, if you have committed a sin in which others were involved, or that led to the sins of others, you have an obligation to make known to your confessor not only the sin itself, but also the scandal you were aware of giving to others. When you confess a sin that involved the mutual consent of another, you need not mention scandal, because your confessor takes it for granted.

After confession, you are bound to do everything in your power to remove any continuing scandal and to repair whatever spiritual

[187] Matt. 18:6-7.

damage you have done to others, because charity binds you to try to save others from sin.

If you have given scandal by bad example, you can correct it by good example and by prayer that the unfortunate impression be corrected. For example, a boy who has led a girl into sin must definitely tell her of his sorrow, of his desire that she, too, seek forgiveness, and of his determination never to be an occasion of sin for her again.

∞

Use delicacy to avoid giving scandal

St. Thomas teaches that things necessary for salvation are not to be omitted, but that the chance of scandalizing the weak obliges us to omit, or at least to defer, words or acts that ordinarily would be permissible until, by a proper explanation, the source of the scandal is removed.

Carefully abstain from things that, although in themselves indifferent or lawful, may, because of circumstances, become to others an occasion of sin. This principle was enjoined by St. Paul regarding the meats offered to idols. Since idols are nothing, these meats were not in themselves forbidden, but, because many Christians believed that they were forbidden, the apostle asked those who were more enlightened to take into account the scruples of their brethren. He said, "Therefore, if food is a cause of my brother's falling, I will never eat meat, lest I cause my brother to fall."[188]

Some people indulge in conversations, reading, styles of dress, and dances that are unbecoming, under the pretext that for them such things have no evil effects. How often they deceive themselves! They scarcely consider the scandal they give to those who

[188] 1 Cor. 8:13.

see their conduct and who take it as an excuse for indulging in pleasures still more dangerous.

Try to foster that delicate sense of charity that may be considered to be the very refinement of the virtue. This is the delicacy advocated by St. Paul. Then the spirit of Christ will dominate you, and your soul will be attuned to tenderness for the spiritual good of those with whom you live. Formal advice, prodding others to "be good," or lording it over them to impress them will make virtue distasteful to those whom you would like to think you have benefitted. If you are not vigilant, even your legitimate good works may become a source of scandal to those less informed than you.

Do not take on what is often called a broad-minded attitude. Others less instructed, who are inclined to break rashly through what they consider to be unnecessary restrictions, use the broadmindedness of those in circumstances similar to theirs to justify their deviations from the straight path of righteousness. They reason, "If excellent Christians can do this, why can't I?" The unfortunate consequence is a sin, for which the broad-minded person may be responsible.

If you have the spirit of Christ, you will realize that your knowledge of moral matters, especially where that knowledge may be likely to be misinterpreted by less informed persons, must be used discreetly. You will then be willing to forgo what would be permitted to you rightly, in order that you may not become a stumbling block to others. Your love for Christ must be so tender and true that you will not open up the way to others to offend Him and thus deprive Him of the fruit of His passion and death. St. Paul says: "By your knowledge this weak man is destroyed, the brother for whom Christ died!"[189]

[189] 1 Cor. 8:11.

The Hidden Power of Kindness

Beg Jesus for love that is strong enough to forgo personal advantage rather than to give occasion to others for sin. Pray also for the special grace of loyalty to Him when, if necessary, you must become a so-called scandal to others, as He had to be on the Cross on Calvary.

∞

Chapter Fifteen

Cultivate a love that overflows in kind deeds

Love is the heart and soul of religion. God is love, and every kind deed is a step toward God. Life is a school in which you acquire knowledge regarding the means of making your life and the lives of your fellowmen happy. That education is founded on love. You cannot live without love, any more than a flower can bloom without sunshine.

There is no power in the world so great as that of love which never loses its strength, never knows its age, and always renews itself. Filial love, fraternal love, conjugal love, patriotism: all are the offshoots of the divine love, rooted in the heart of Jesus, which broke in death so that it might bring love to the world.

Love seeks to assert itself by deeds. Love, a very real force, is not content with fair words. The effect of love is an eagerness to be up and doing, to heal, to serve, to give, to shelter, and to console. A love that remains inactive, a force that is asleep, is a dying love. If you do not wish to cease to love, you must never cease to do good.

Because a kind thought inspires a kind deed, it is a real blessing. A kind word spoken or a harsh word withheld has spelled happiness for many a burdened soul. To have acquired the ability not to think and speak uncharitably of others is a great achievement. The habit of interpreting the conduct of others favorably is one of the finer qualities of charity, but the highest charity is evidenced by doing good to others. Greater than a kind thought, more refreshing than a kind word, is the union of thought and word in action. St. Augustine says, "We are what our works are. According as our works are good or bad, we are good or bad; for we are the trees, and our works the fruit. It is by the fruit that one judges of the quality of the tree."

The highest perfection of charity consists in laying down one's life for another, just as Christ offered His life as a sacrifice for mankind.

The Savior once said, "Not everyone who says to me, 'Lord, Lord' shall enter the kingdom of Heaven, but he who does the will of my Father who is in Heaven."[190] And the heavenly Father expressed His will in the great commandments: "Thou shalt love the Lord thy God. . . . Thou shalt love thy neighbor as thyself."[191]

Our Lord wants your life to be love in action, even as His was, for He said, "This is my commandment, that you love one another as I have loved you."[192] St. Peter summarizes His life in the words: "He went about doing good."[193]

St. Thérèse of the Child Jesus said, "It is not enough that I should give to whosoever may ask of me; I must forestall their desires and show that I feel much gratified, much honored, in rendering service; and if they take a thing that I use, I must seem as

---

[190] Matt. 7:21.

[191] Matt. 22:37, 39 (Douay-Rheims edition).

[192] John 15:12.

[193] Acts 10:38.

though glad to be relieved of it. . . . To let our thoughts dwell upon self renders the soul sterile; we must quickly turn to labors of love."

Love is the heart and soul of kind deeds. Just as there is no charity without works, so there may be works of charity without love. St. Paul expressed it this way: "If I give away all I have, and if I deliver my body to be burned, but have not love, I gain nothing."[194]

Some people use charity as an effective cloak to hide their human weaknesses. Cowardice, for instance, is being afraid of what people will say. Some people will do a certain amount of good out of sheer cowardice, while in the meantime their avarice covers itself with the cloak of charity.

Self-interest, greed, and vanity also borrow the cloak of charity. Since charitable works draw popular attention, they are bound to prove an excellent advertisement. If a man's past hinders his social success, he hastens to put on the cloak of charity which literally "covers a multitude of sins."[195]

Pride and the love of power sometimes put on the cloak of charity, for it gives a man a noble appearance. The demon of pride once was willing to give all his possessions to Christ if, falling down, He would adore him.[196]

Others take up the practice of charity as a kind of sport. They look for the exhilarating feeling of having done a good deed. Later there will be material for selfish conversation.

God is not content with the cloak of charity, or mere kind deeds. He looks for genuine goodness and love. The day will come when He will take away the borrowed cloak of kindness.

[194] 1 Cor. 13:3.
[195] 1 Pet. 4:8.
[196] Cf. Matt. 4:9.

God does not so much desire that we should cooperate with Him in His works of mercy as that we should participate in His sincere and ever-active love. His law of social duty is not "Thou shalt give to thy neighbor," but "Thou shalt love thy neighbor."

∞

Strive for goodness, not just good deeds

Realizing that God sees all, examine your charitable undertakings and diligently look into your motives. Reject what is meant to pass for charity but is not real love. It is far better to do less "good" and to have more goodness. Lay aside the mere cloak of charity, and, in its place, according to the beautiful words of the apostle, "put on . . . compassion, kindness, lowliness, meekness, and patience."[197] That means to cultivate a heart full of genuine, sincere kindness. Then you will be able to appear arrayed in the nuptial garment in the presence of Him who is everlasting love and truth. "The Son of Man is to come with His angels in the glory of His Father, and then He will repay every man for what he has done."[198]

Charity, to be real, must be strong, energetic, and abundant. It must be replenished constantly. Its abundance is the measure and proof of a vigorous spiritual life.

St. Paul assured the early Christians that he prayed not only for *some* charity for his converts but for abundant charity. He would have no limits, no measure. He was convinced that Christ's followers should have a burning zeal to practice charity, this queen of virtues. He says, "It is my prayer that your love may abound more and more, with knowledge and all discernment."[199]

[197] Col. 3:12.
[198] Matt. 16:27.
[199] Phil. 1:9.

He states that this charity should not be pursued blindly, but should be accompanied with a full "knowledge and all discernment." Love without reason, without discrimination, is false charity. Such love is weakness and may even be very harmful. Charity enlightened with the truth of God and the understanding of the things that are of genuine spiritual value will effect great holiness in your life.

Self-glorification is a rather pagan attitude of mind. Christlike love of self, to which we all are called in virtue of our vocation to the true faith, should urge us to rise to the higher levels of the love of God. It is ultimately to your own advantage to acquire a proficiency in serving God with the sole intention of pleasing Him alone.

Man can resist force, reasoning, science, and talent, but if someone does good to him, he will yield, and all the more readily if the charity is based on a supernatural motive. Sometimes the person who performed the good deed never sees its fulfillment; God wishes to add this sacrifice to the merits of His apostolic zeal. But sooner or later, love will be triumphant. Love always succeeds.

Chapter Sixteen

∽

Perform works of mercy

The object of all love is the good of the one loved. The object of love of God is the honor and glory of God; the object of love of neighbor is the spiritual and temporal welfare of your fellowmen and, through that, the honor and glory of God. You must love your neighbor for God's sake.

The love of neighbor imposes many duties upon you, directed toward your neighbor's well-being and happiness.

Your first duty is to give material help to your neighbor whenever possible. Jesus said, "For I was hungry, and you gave me food; I was thirsty, and you gave me drink. I was naked, and you clothed me."[200] Although this is only assistance for the body, it is nonetheless necessary.

The chief corporal works of mercy are: to feed the hungry, to give drink to the thirsty, to clothe the naked, to visit the imprisoned, to shelter the homeless, to visit the sick, and to bury the dead.

Almsgiving in a truly Christian manner not only allays temporal want, but raises the spirit of the poor above their depressing

---

[200] Matt. 25:35, 36.

wants and difficulties. The spirit of love should transform the world and make it a better place in which to live. Poverty will never be entirely eliminated, but there need not always be so much poverty that easily could be lessened in the measure in which each one of us is able to diminish it.

Thus St. John says, "But if anyone has the world's goods and sees his brother in need, yet closes his heart against him, how does God's love abide in him? Little children, let us not love in word or speech but in deed and in truth."[201]

St. Paul expresses the true Christian attitude in this respect. "As for the rich in this world, charge them not to be haughty, nor to set their hopes on uncertain riches, but on God, who richly furnishes us with everything to enjoy. They are to do good, to be rich in good deeds, liberal and generous, thus laying up for themselves a good foundation for the future, so that they may take hold of the life which is life indeed."[202]

The Church has always defended the right of private property. But the surplus, before adding to the rich man's abundance, should go to those who lack the necessities of life. When a rich man is disliked, it is not because of his wealth, but because he is making bad use of it. Not the rich owner, but the man who has an exaggerated love for the goods of this world, grieves our Lord.

Give of what you have. After all, it is not really yours. Goods of this world are only borrowed from God. You are bound to use and to distribute them according to God's will. It is not he who possesses much who is rich, but he who gives away much. To keep things you own away from those in need, in opposition to God's will, has all the earmarks of robbery. And St. Paul says, "Do not

[201] 1 John 3:17-18.
[202] 1 Tim. 6:17-19.

err: neither . . . thieves, nor covetous . . . nor extortioners . . . shall possess the kingdom of God."[203]

St. Vincent de Paul said, "Oh, how great was the love Jesus Christ had for the poor! He chose the state of poverty, He is the Father of the poor, He considers as done for Himself what is done for them. It is proper, then, to love the poor with a special love, seeing in them the person of Jesus Christ, and doing all for them as if done for Him."

∞

Christ calls you to visit the sick

An important corporal work of mercy is visiting the sick. Some may be able to live without the love of their fellowmen, but the love of others is the very life of the sick.

Sick people, who need as much love as children, are often hard to love. They are often ill-tempered, discontented, sensitive, exacting, and selfish.

Nevertheless, sickness brings out many a lovable feature in a person. In sickness, a man becomes once more a man, stripped of official garb and externals of position and honor. Whatever he may have been, upon a bed of suffering he becomes like any simple child in need of help. Sickness makes people more simple and humble.

A kind of divine radiance plays over the poor human features of a sick person, for, in some way, he resembles the suffering Christ, outwardly disfigured so that "He had no form or comeliness that we should look at Him, and no beauty that we should desire Him."[204] Perhaps inwardly he is sad, as Christ was when He

[203] 1 Cor. 6:9-10 (Douay-Rheims edition).
[204] Isa. 53:2.

said, "My soul is very sorrowful, even to death."[205] There is nothing that the sick suffer that Christ has not suffered before him.

The sick person may claim charity as a sacred right. His sufferings must not be increased by lack of consideration and understanding, by noise and talk. And yet he is not to be left to himself in his misery.

Go to a sick person and serve him in any way you can, either by a word of comfort and encouragement, or by conversation, or by nursing him, or by some gift or pleasant surprise. The fine tactfulness of love will enable you to avoid letting the sufferer feel that it costs you an effort to stay with him.

Remember that visiting and tending the sick is a work of mercy by which you relieve the sufferer from some small portion of his misery by sharing it with him. When the sick person, rendered irritable by suffering and robbed by it of his self-control, wishes to speak out, listen to him, if by so doing you can ease his mind.

Even if the sick person is inconsiderate, demanding now this, and now that, render him these services if they comfort him. When you enter a sickroom, diffuse as much cheerfulness, calm, and patience as you can. Remember that even a drink of water given to the sick is given to Him who on the Cross cried out, "I thirst."[206]

Christ Himself, the model of those who visit and care for the sick, did not readily forgo actual contact with the sick. Thus He touched a diseased eye, a diseased ear and tongue, and laid His hand upon lepers.[207] Jesus knew well what a comfort it is to the sick not to be overlooked.

[205] Matt. 26:38.
[206] John 19:28.
[207] Matt. 9:29; Mark 7:33; Matt. 8:3.

St. Vincent de Paul says, "It is a work most agreeable to our Savior to visit the sick and infirm, and to comfort them, as He Himself recommended this kind of mercy. But to perform it with greater zeal and merit, you must see Jesus Christ in the person of the sick, for Jesus Christ says He will regard as done to Him what we do for the poor and infirm."

Once St. John of the Cross[208] was washing the feet of a humble beggar, when suddenly there appeared on the feet he was washing the stigmata of our Lord. Unperturbed and with utter simplicity, the saint looked up into the beggar's eyes and said, "So it is You, Lord."

If you had no time for the sick, will Jesus not have reason to look at you reproachfully at your judgment and complain in the name of all the neglected sick: "I was sick and in prison, and you did not visit me"?[209]

Suffering humanity is calling out to you, clamoring for a kind deed. If sorrow becomes bearable to you, let it be the sorrow of your neighbor. In imitation of Jesus, you should always be ready to do good deeds, even when they are not obligatory. You are obliged, however, to perform the works of mercy in the name of Christ, according to your ability and the need of your neighbor.

∞

Tend to the spiritual needs of others

Your second duty is to give spiritual help to your neighbor whenever possible. More distressing than bodily wants are the ills of the spirit. The chief spiritual works of mercy are: to admonish

---

[208] St. John of the Cross (1542-1591), mystical Doctor and cofounder of the Discalced Carmelites.
[209] Matt. 25:43.

the sinner, to instruct the ignorant, to counsel the doubtful, to comfort the sorrowful, to bear wrongs patiently, to forgive all injuries, and to pray for the living and the dead.

Nothing in this world is so precious as a soul in grace, because it was bought by the precious blood of Christ. A lifetime spent in rescuing only one soul from spiritual ruin is a life well spent. If circumstances do not permit you to deal with many souls, be devoted to the few that a loving Providence has placed near you.

Doing good to others is a selfless charity. Sharing the physical and material needs of others, lessening their hardships, soothing their heartaches, and being instrumental in obtaining spiritual aid for their souls is Christlike charity. All such charity is contributing to the welfare of the Mystical Body of Christ, the Church.

In the world today, besides bodily misery, there is much misery of the soul — dying faith, shattered hope, crushed love, doubt, error, passion, and sin. Do not let your charity heedlessly pass over such misery.

One day the people laid at the feet of Jesus a man cruelly sick of the palsy. But our Lord saw in him a much more cruel misery — the sickness of the soul. Touched with divine compassion, He spoke an omnipotent word, "Take heart, my son; your sins are forgiven."[210] Our Lord saw that the need of the sick man's soul was far greater than that of his body.

The soul is more keenly aware of its needs than the body. One who suffers only in his body may be happy, so long as his soul is healthy. But one whose soul is sick can never be at rest, no matter how well he may be in body. The sinner is not always aware of his sickness. But the sinner's wretched condition does not end peacefully with his death; it begins then in real earnest.

[210] Matt. 9:2.

∞

Kind deeds lead souls to Christ

On another occasion, Jesus beheld the wretched misery of a woman taken in adultery and He was moved to pity. He saw a human soul, His Father's most beautiful and most noble creature, a child of God, and He turned to this soul in compassionate love and said, "Neither do I condemn you."[211] In these words there is compassion, confidence, love, and readiness to help. The sinner needs not judgment but mercy and kindness. Kindness has converted more sinners than zeal, eloquence, or learning.

Unless you are a priest in the confessional, you cannot speak a word to release the sinner from his spiritual misery, but you have the power of kind speech. A good word, prudently and lovingly spoken, has a wonderful force. You also have the silent yet most eloquent language of good example that speaks louder than words. Lastly, you have the mighty word of prayer, by which you can save the souls of men by securing grace for their conversion.

Make use of these words, even as Christ made use of His mighty words. You have a mission in life to reconquer for God His unhappy and disobedient world and turn it back to Him. You perform a wonderful act of charity for the sinner when you help free him from the misery of sin in order to put him on the road to God's own peace and everlasting life.

But you can also do a service to God, who is always near the sinner and makes the sinner's interests His very own. The sinner was created in God's image and likeness, but now this sacred and beautiful image is distorted and desecrated by sin. You should feel urged to restore the likeness of God in the soul of the sinner. You must help, if you are at all able to help.

[211] John 8:11.

But it is not only the image of God that suffers in the sinner; in a certain sense, God Himself is dishonored and even crucified, as St. Paul says, "They crucify the Son of God on their own account and hold Him up to contempt."[212]

It is a glorious deed to convert a sinner and, as it were, draw the nails from the hands and feet of his God nailed to the wood of sin and suffering in the soul of a sinner.

This is also a splendid service *done to yourself*. As a child of eternity, you are conscious of a craving to work for eternity. This longing of your soul will be fully satisfied if you lend a hand in the work of the salvation of souls. St. Ignatius Loyola gives this advice: "I counsel you to devote yourself to aiding the soul of your neighbor in such a manner that you may always have for your own the care that is fitting to preserve it and to perfect it in every kind of virtue, to the glory of our Lord God."

---

[212] Heb. 6:6.

∞

Chapter Seventeen

Reap the rewards of kind deeds

By now, you probably realize with consternation that there are many phases of charity in which you not only do not abound, but are seriously lacking in even minimum requirements.

Begin by being rich in charitable thoughts. The constant exercise of thinking kindly and excusingly of those who annoy or cross or pain you will put you well on the way to lessening your faults against charity. An overflowing surplus of charitable thoughts will make you more charitable in word and act.

∞

Kind deeds will make you holy

Kind deeds for the love of God have the power to make you truly holy.

• *Kindness makes you a friend of Jesus,* for He said, "This is my commandment, that you love one another as I love you."[213] Kindness is a sharing in the spirit of Jesus, which is itself the life of all holiness.

[213] John 15:12.

Kindness will make you a devoted child of God, as Jesus reminds you, "Love your enemies and pray for those who persecute you, so that you may be sons of your Father who is in Heaven."[214] And St. John says, "Beloved, let us love one another, for love is of God, and he who loves is born of God and knows God. He who does not love does not know God; for God is love."[215] St. John implies that love of your neighbor is but another form of the love of God,[216] and St. Paul teaches that love is the fulfillment of the law.[217]

• *Kind deeds lead you to God.* Every step you take on the road of kindness is a long stride toward God. St. John Climacus[218] once remarked, "Every creature is a ladder to raise us to God."

• *Kind actions help to get rid of your selfishness.* Since kind actions depend upon unselfish motives, they tend to form habits of disinterestedness, which prepare you for the highest motives of divine love. Selfishness must be put down, or your progress to union with God and virtue will cease.

Kind actions teach you to be generous in making sacrifices. Like God's goodness, they are constantly occupied where there is no hope of being repaid. As God always acts for His own glory, so kind actions, when they are habitual, are very frequently done for Him alone and have a way of

---

[214] Matt. 5:44.

[215] 1 John 4:7-8.

[216] 1 John 4:7-12, 19.

[217] Rom. 13:8.

[218] St. John Climacus (c. 570-c. 649), acestic and writer on the spiritual life.

remaining hidden. God often rewards them by arranging that they remain unrepaid so that you may look only to Him for your reward.

Thus, kindness is the easiest road to humility, and perhaps the surest. A proud man is seldom a kind man. Humility makes you kind, and kindness makes you humble. Much grace goes along with kindness — grace sufficient to make you a saint.

• *Kindness imparts true wisdom.* St. James says, "The wisdom from above is first pure, then peaceable, gentle, open to reason, full of mercy and good fruits, without uncertainty or insincerity. And the harvest of righteousness is sown in peace by those who make peace."[219]

The wisdom that love bestows on man is not ordinary, but is "from above." The world has a philosophy that, unmindful of the pain or joy of mankind, has no other interest but the solution of its own problems. St. Paul says, "And if I have prophetic powers, and understand all mysteries and all knowledge, and if I have all faith, so as to remove mountains, but have not love, I am nothing."[220]

You possess true wisdom if you practice charity. Perfect wisdom is more than words; it is action and life. The warmth of the heart turns almost spontaneously into light and guidance for the mind. A truly kind man will never be so narrow in his judgments as one who has no charity, however gifted or educated he may be. By love, man is raised above the troubles and needs of his existence so that he views things with a wide and comprehensive glance. The

[219] James 3:17-18.
[220] 1 Cor. 13:2.

saints, even those who were lowly and simple, have often had a strangely clear and farseeing eye for questions of divine and human knowledge. St. John says, "He who loves his brother abides in the light, and in it there is not cause for stumbling."[221]

The kinder a man is, the closer he draws to the wisdom of eternal Love. We might even say that love is nothing but one of God's thoughts, the depth of which is unknown and unsuspected by reason, living on in the heart of man.

Fr. Faber writes, "But so much we are warranted in saying that charity is the deepest view of life, and nearest to God's view, and therefore also, not merely the truest view, but the only view which is true at all. Kind thoughts, then, are in the creature what His science is to the Creator. They embody the deepest, purest, grandest truth, to which we untruthful creatures can attain about others or ourselves."[222]

• *Life is the greatest and most precious reward of charity*, and the greatest and deepest yearning of man is life — an ever-growing, deeper, endless life. What men call life — eating, sleeping, hurrying, idling, enjoying, and wanting — is not life at all. Neither does life become stronger and richer by mere thinking, dreaming, or reading. The experience of beauty does not really deepen or enrich our life. Every sensation gives us something and takes away something of our vital energy.

Natural life, even though it is a gift of love and is ever strengthened by it, does not suffice by itself. Purely natural

[221] 1 John 2:10.
[222] Faber, *Spiritual Conferences*, 41.

life will one day come to an end. Love alone makes life fuller and stronger.

There is a supernatural life of the soul, an immortal existence. St. John often speaks of "eternal life" and "being born of God" and draws attention to the intimate connection between that life and charity. "We know that we have passed out of death into life, because we love the brethren. He who does not love remains in death."[223]

Charity has many things in common with the divine life. Like God's own life, it is not under the sway of time. All the plans, thoughts, and actions of the eternal life of God are eternal love. St. Paul says, "Love never ends; as for prophecies, they will pass away; as for tongues, they will cease; as for knowledge, it will pass away."[224]

Although the supernatural life of the soul is not identical with the habit of charity poured into us by God, love of God and our neighbor is an indispensable condition for obtaining this supernatural life, as well as for its maintenance and increase. Love alone may say, "I believe in eternal life." Only one who loves both God and man has life in him. That life is like a seed that, although it must one day be hidden in the dark earth, will surely wake up again — to eternal light.

Among the rewards of generous charity that St. Paul lists are these: high appreciation of spiritual values, great purity of life, easy judgment at death, and a large sharing in the glorification and praise of God in Heaven throughout eternity. He says, "It is my prayer that . . . you may approve what is excellent, and may be

[223] 1 John 3:14.
[224] 1 Cor. 13:8.

pure and blameless for the day of Christ, filled with the fruits of righteousness which comes through Jesus Christ, to the glory and praise of God."[225]

The rewards of charity that St. Paul mentions are worth meditating on.

First, he prays, "that you may approve what is excellent." By the very exercise of charity, your concept of the requirements of Christian perfection will become more definite. Striving for holiness will become more important and more attractive.

Second, he prays, "that you may be pure and blameless." Genuine charity will enable you to avoid sin. Great purity in life follows inevitably upon sincerity of conscience.

Third, he promises those who are rich in charity such sustaining aid of grace that they will so triumph over the hindrances met with in daily life that they will be "pure and blameless for the day of Christ" — on the Day of Judgment, when Christ will gain His ultimate victory over sin.

Fourth, he claims that they will be "filled with the fruits of righteousness which come through Jesus Christ." This fruit consists in the holiness that you will attain by cooperation with the graces you have received, that you may give "glory and praise" to God in Heaven.

Such excellent and far-reaching rewards of charity ought to be strong incentives to make you want to have charity dominate your life as far as possible.

Ask Jesus that on the Day of Judgment He may lead you "to the glory and praise of God," His Father, especially because you have been rich in charity. Ask for an ever-finer discerning love for your neighbor.

[225] Phil. 1:9-11.

∞

God's blessing accompanies every kind deed

God always helps those who help others to help themselves. Our Lord promised that even a cup of cold water given in His name would not go without its reward. If, then, you are kind to God's children — who are your brothers and sisters in the family of God — God will be kind to you. Everything you do for others without any thought of yourself, you really do for yourself. A wise saying of the Old Testament is: "Cast your bread upon the waters, for you will find it after many days."[226]

At the hands of God, love will receive the best and most precious of rewards: His love. If love could never fail to find an echo on earth, it would surely find one in Heaven. St. John says, "No man has ever seen God; if we love one another, God abides in us; His love is perfected in us."[227]

If the Heavenly Father loves every one of His creatures, even the greatest sinner, He surely loves most those who, by their kind thoughts and actions, prove themselves in a special manner His children. The Son of God must have a very special love for those who fulfill His most earnest wish, for He says, "If you keep my commandments, you will abide in my love, just as I have kept my Father's love commandments and abide in His love."[228]

The Holy Spirit, the Spirit of divine love, is specially drawn to those whose souls are animated by His Spirit and burn with the fire of His divine love.

If you love your neighbor and prove it by kind deeds, you will have a special place in the heart of the Blessed Trinity, and the

[226] Eccles. 11:1.
[227] 1 John 4:12.
[228] John 15:10.

three divine Persons will take delight in dwelling in your soul, as Jesus promised: "If a man loves me, he will keep my word, and my Father will love him, and we will come to him and make our home with him."[229]

God will bless you not only outwardly with His benefits, but, above all, inwardly with His grace. If the saints preserved rich graces throughout their life and merited a constant increase of them, it was surely because of their earnest love for their neighbor.

Sometimes God will almost let you feel His invisible love deep in your soul, and let you enjoy the sweetness of His wonderful nearness, because of your charity to your fellowmen. This sense of the nearness of God is the highest and keenest joy that can be tasted upon earth. It is the hour when our Lord fulfills His promise: "He who loves me will be loved by my Father, and I will love him and manifest myself to him."[230] There is hardly a better means of passing from darkness to light — from a sense of separation to a feeling of God's nearness — than to fulfill God's command of charity.

If you are kind, you will never be forsaken by God. His love will be visible in the many blessings you receive. The psalmist says, "Blessed is he who considers the poor! The Lord delivers him in the day of trouble; the Lord protects him and keeps him alive; he is called blessed in the land; Thou dost not give him up to the will of his enemies. The Lord sustains him on his sickbed; in his illness Thou healest all his infirmities."[231]

Nothing is truer than that God's love rewards as generously as He has promised: "Give, and it will be given to you; good measure,

[229] John 14:23.
[230] John 14:21.
[231] Ps. 41:1-3.

pressed down, shaken together, running over, will be put into your lap. For the measure you give will be the measure you get back."[232]

∞

Kind deeds are a source of happiness

Interior happiness almost always follows a kind action. Happiness of the soul is the atmosphere in which great things are done for God. You will be truly happy if God's love dominates your life and enables you to love your neighbor. You may be the poorest of creatures, yet you will have secured the best thing in life. St. John says, "He who loves his brother abides in the light." When you practice charity, your soul will be flooded with the sunshine of happiness.

Faithful, self-forgetting service, love that spends itself over and over, is the secret of true happiness. Happiness is a mosaic composed of many smaller stones. The little acts of kindness, the little courtesies, are the things that, added up at night, constitute the secret of a happy day.

Try to make at least one person happy every day. Every morning build a booth to shelter someone from life's fierce heat. If you cannot do a kind deed, speak a kind word. If you cannot speak a kind word, think a kind thought. Count up, if you can, the treasure of happiness that you would dispense in a week, in a year, in a lifetime!

There is perhaps nothing that counts for more in life, and the memory of which lasts longer and more blessedly, than just that simple quality of heart: kindness. If you sow deeds of kindness, you will have a perpetual harvest. The best portion of your life is the little nameless acts of kindness and love. Endeavor so to regulate

[232] Luke 6:38.

231

your life in kindness that your name will be carved in the hearts of those with whom you come in contact, rather than upon a marble slab for strangers to read.

∞

Kind deeds merit the forgiveness of sins

Forgiveness of sin and brotherly love are closely linked together. The pardon of sin is one of the most sublime rewards of charity. St. Peter says, "Above all, hold unfailing your love for one another, since love covers a multitude of sins."[233]

Charity plays a great role before the tribunal of God. The sacrament of Penance has no efficacy if there is no love in the heart of the penitent. On the other hand, by love alone many venial sins may be expiated, and a large part of the claims of divine justice may be satisfied without confession.

Of all the works of penance you may perform — in connection with the sacrament of Penance or independently of it — works of charity are surely those that give most satisfaction to God, offer the greatest edification to the world, and obtain the highest spiritual profit for yourself. St. James says, "My brethren, if anyone among you wanders from the truth and someone brings him back, let him know that whoever brings back a sinner from the error of his way will save his soul from death and will cover a multitude of sins."[234]

After confession, never fail to perform some act of charity as a sign of your good will. Each night perform a kindly deed, such as expressing a sincere desire to forgive and forget injuries or saying a prayer to God for those who may have injured you.

[233] 1 Pet. 4:8.
[234] James 5:19-20.

The hour of death will be a most unwelcome one to him who was a stranger to charity and compassion during his lifetime. But a man whose heart is full of goodness and love will be admitted into God's kingdom of love. God's eye will not rest upon his weakness and sinfulness, but, rather, upon his charity and good deeds. St. James says, "For judgment is without mercy to one who has shown no mercy; yet mercy triumphs over judgment."[235]

Apart from avoiding mortal sin, you can prepare for the hour of death in no better way than to foster in your heart the spirit of love, which will almost force you to practice kind thoughts, words, and deeds. Our Lord said, "Blessed are the merciful, for they shall obtain mercy."[236]

∞

You owe much to the kind deeds of others

Think how much you yourself owe to kind actions. If you look back through the years, you will be amazed to consider the number of kind deeds that have been done for you. They are almost beyond your counting. Those you remember are hardly so numerous as those you have forgotten, not through ingratitude, but because of the distractions of life and the limits of your memory.

Kind deeds have been done for you under various circumstances. They have come to you, with blame as well as with praise, from unexpected persons. They have made you joyful in the midst of your tears. Every one of these acts of kindness has certainly done you some spiritual good. If they did not make you better at the time, they prepared the way for your becoming better, or they sowed a seed of future goodness by making an impression whose

[235] James 2:13.
[236] Matt. 5:7.

power you never suspected. Time and again, kindness has done the preliminary work for grace in your soul. In fact, all this kindness was a special form of grace.

Think of how little you have deserved all the kind actions that you have received from God and your fellow creatures. You have surely received more kindness yourself than you have shown to others. Perhaps the thought of all the kindness of so many persons sometimes becomes almost painful, because of the realization of your own unkindness. People have done the work of angels in your behalf. They have encouraged you to do good. And what actually have you done?

It is frightening to think what you would have been, had parents, friends, teachers, and schoolmates been less kind to you. All through life, kindness may have been bridling the tendency to evil that was in you. This recollection of it now should be one of your greatest incentives to practice virtue. Realizing that you owe all this to the kindness of others should urge you to do all in your power to make kindness the golden rule of your life.

∞

You will be judged according to your kindness

You will be judged and will gain merit in Heaven according to the spiritual and corporal works of mercy you perform for the love of God. In the Day of Judgment, our Lord will use the performance of the spiritual and corporal works of mercy as a name to distinguish the elect from the wicked. "Then the King will say to those at his right hand, 'Come, O blessed of my Father, inherit the kingdom prepared for you from the foundation of the world.' " And then He will give the reason: "For I was hungry, and you gave me food; I was thirsty, and you gave me drink; I was a stranger, and you welcomed me; I was naked, and you clothed me; I was sick, and you visited me; I was in prison, and you came to me." And the just will wonder, for never have they seen our Lord in such need. But He will answer them, "Truly, I say to you, as you did it to one of the least of these my brethren, you did it to me."[237] Afterward he will dismiss the wicked forever from Himself, because they have not loved Him in the person of His brethren. Thus from the mouth of Jesus Himself we know that our eternal lot will be founded on the love we have had for Him in the person of our brethren.

It is remarkable that Christ, in telling us of the coming judgment, makes the final destiny of all men depend upon whether they have, in this world, exercised the virtue of kindness. Those who neglect the works of mercy He will reproach; His eternal curse will be their portion. Neglect of love's duties is a sin quite as serious and far-reaching in its consequences as the direct doing of things that are wrong in themselves.

So when you appear before Christ on the last day, He will not ask you if you have passed your life in penance and fasting, if you have given many hours of prayer, but if you have loved and helped your neighbor. Other commandments are certainly not to be put aside, but your observance of them will have served for nothing if you have not kept this commandment of loving your neighbor, which is so dear to Christ's Sacred Heart.

∞

Heaven is love's reward

The reward that God bestows on us during life on earth is only a foretaste of the reward that He has in store for us at the end of our life. Heaven is the final and full reward by which God repays us for all the good we have done upon earth.

[237] Matt. 25:34-36, 40.

Heaven is something of God's very own bliss — a drop from God's own joy, a drop of bliss out of God's own heart. On earth, love is often rewarded with many a drop of bitterness, such as ingratitude, meanness, misinterpretation of motives, and abuse of kindness. But in eternity, a sweetness will fill the whole soul.

Heaven is something of God's glory. Here on earth, goodness, the heart's highest nobility, does not win a very large share of the honors lavished on genius, aristocracy, or popularity. But in eternity, a kind soul receives its due reward. The book of Wisdom describes this reward: "Their reward is with the Lord; the Most High takes care of them. Therefore they will receive a glorious crown and a beautiful diadem from the hand of the Lord."[238]

Then all those who have fulfilled the great law of the divine Teacher here below shall be permitted to have part in the glory of the Father and the Son, according to the prayer of Jesus: "The glory which Thou hast given me I have given to them, that they may be one even as we are one, I in them and Thou in me, that they may be perfectly one."[239]

On earth, the kind man has sacrificed much time in order to serve, to help, and to oblige his neighbor. By toil, privation, and forgetfulness of self, many have even shortened their lives by months or even years, after the example of incarnate Love: "By this we know love, that He laid down His life for us; and we ought to lay down our lives for the brethren."[240]

But the reward for love is an eternity in which to live, to love, and to rejoice in love's activities. "Love never ends."[241] As God

---

[238] Wisd. 5:15-16.
[239] John 17:22-23.
[240] 1 John 3:16.
[241] 1 Cor. 13:8.

outlives all that lives, so does charity outlive all things — the power, science, art, and beauty of this world. The charitable man also lives forever, for Heaven is a bit of God's eternity.

Heaven is the possession of God Himself. To every good and kind soul, God says, "I am thy . . . reward exceeding great."[242] And St. John speaks in the same fashion: "He who keeps his commandments abides in God and God in him."[243] Everlasting Love gives itself to the person who, while on earth, gives his poor human love to his brethren. You carry eternal love in your soul, with its tremendous wealth and bliss — a life of endless existence. If human love is great, the divine and everlasting Love is a million times greater, like the blazing sun compared with a flickering candle.

Our Lord will not let Himself be outdone in generosity, and He will, in return for your acts of charity, grant you many graces for the services done to Him in the person of His least brethren. In the family of God, we all are brothers and sisters with Jesus as our elder Brother. Each time you are kind, you do a service to Jesus; at the same time, Jesus acts in your soul by His grace to make it more beautiful and holy. But His greatest reward to you will be an imperishable store of merit in His kingdom and, above all, the eternal possession of Him. You will possess the God of love for having loved Him in the person of your neighbor.

St. Catherine of Genoa[244] once said, "If men only knew in what manner our Lord will reward in the other world the good we do here, our understanding, our memory, and our will would be occupied only with good works, no matter what it might cost to perform them."

---

[242] Gen. 15:1 (Douay-Rheims edition).
[243] Cf. 1 John 3:24.
[244] St. Catherine of Genoa (1447-1510), mystic.

Therefore, you have every reason to rejoice as you look forward to the reward that awaits you for your kindness and considerateness, your willingness to help, your unselfishness, generosity, and gentleness. St. John says, "We know that we have passed out of death into life, because we love the brethren." And the Lord Himself tells you, "Rejoice and be glad, for your reward is great in Heaven."[245]

[245] Matt. 5:12.

How kind are you?

∞

Kind Thoughts

Have I refused in my heart to forgive
a person who has injured me?

Have I recalled, when hurt by others, how God has forgiven me
for my sins and tried to forgive in the same generous spirit?

Have I nursed resentment against others,
even though I did make an effort at forgiveness?

Has my sensitiveness caused me to be unfriendly toward others?

Have I cast a gloom over my surroundings
by giving way to morose and sullen moods?

Have I permitted jealousy toward another to show in my conduct?

Do I deliberately harbor unkind and
revengeful thoughts about others?

Have I attributed bad motives to others,
when I could not be certain of their motives?

Am I inclined to be rude, impolite, distant, or harsh in my judgments?

The Hidden Power of Kindness

Have I been sufficiently aware of the far-reaching power
of my example, which influences others for good or
bad, even when I do not advert to that influence?

Do I frequently remember these words of Christ,
which apply to acts of charity: "As you did it to one
of the least of these my brethren, you did it to me"?

Do I wish my neighbor all the good things that I wish for myself?

Have I adopted the twofold motto: "Never give pain,
and promote the happiness of others whenever possible"?

∞

Kind Words

As a husband or wife, have I made an
effort to prevent the sins of my spouse?

Have I neglected my duty of preventing those in my charge
from committing sin, or correcting them after they have failed?

Have I failed to report to someone in authority the certain
sins of a neighbor that I knew were doing harm to innocent
persons or to the community as a whole?

Have I refused to talk to or recognize someone who has wronged me?

When I was guilty of doing evil against my neighbor, have I refused in
word or in deed to show that I was sorry and wished to be forgiven?

After a quarrel with another, have I refused to make
any advances toward reconciliation?

Have I, by silence or approval, failed to prevent the
defamation of another's character when I could have done so?

Have I permitted gossip and petty talebearing to go on in
my presence, without making an effort to change the subject?

How kind are you?

Have I evaded an opportunity to
enlighten someone on religious truth?

Have I slandered others by attributing to them sins that
they did not commit or of which I had no evidence?

Is an absent person's reputation safe when I am
present, or do I join in the discussion of his faults?

Have I ruined the reputation of others by telling their
secret sins to persons who could not otherwise have known
them and who had no claim to such information?

Have I lied in order that I might gain from another's loss?

Have I destroyed or lessened the faith of others by speaking
contemptuously about religion, the Church, priests, and so forth?

Have I engaged in petty gossip about my neighbors?

Have I told my friends the unkind remarks others
made about them and, in this way, occasioned ill will?

Have I made cutting and sarcastic remarks to others?

Do I watch my words and conduct, especially
when in the presence of children, since I know
how easily they imitate older people?

Am I a chronic complainer by habitually looking
for flaws and pointing them out to others?

Are my murmurings the outcome of wounded pride or self-will?

Do I enter generously into the joys of others, or do
I put a damper on them by my adverse attitude?

Do I complain about the weather, my boss,
or the people I work with or live with?

Do I complain about the work I have to do?

Am I a kind listener?

Can I listen to the same story or the same stale
jokes, without making the speaker aware of my
annoyance by breaking in or cutting him short?

Can I offer words of praise readily?

Do I begrudge the words of praise I hear addressed to others,
especially if these words are to the credit of someone I do not
particularly like, or of whom I may be somewhat jealous?

, Have I formed the habit of offering a ready
thank-you for small favors received?

Do I ever make an effort to say encouraging words?

Do I check my impulses to reply to unkind words
in a spirit of revenge or to defend myself?

∽

Kind Deeds

Have I tried to deepen my faith regarding
the truth that every act of charity toward a
neighbor is also an act of love of God?

Have I refused to give alms for the relief of the
needy or to charitable causes, such as the missions, even
though I had opportunities and sufficient means without
depriving myself or my family of the necessities of life?

Have I measured my charity only by what others gave,
or by what I might receive in return, instead of by my
ability to give and by the need of others?

Have I faced the truth that I shall take no material wealth
with me beyond death, and that the memory and merit of
deeds of charity will then be my greatest consolation?

How kind are you?

Have I demanded publicity and praise for my almsgiving?

Have I squandered or given away money outside my home to the extent that it left my immediate family in want of necessary things? Have I been remiss in my duty toward the sick who were dependent on me?

Have I cooperated with another in committing a sin?

When I had the opportunity, have I done anything to prevent evil, such as the circulation of obscene books and magazines?

Have I led others, especially children,
into sin by suggestion or bad example?

Have I permitted another to suffer injustice or
mistreatment when my influence could have prevented it?

Have I rejected opportunities to comfort someone in
sorrow, or to encourage someone in danger of despair?

Have I sought opportunities to revenge myself
on others by inflicting pain on them?

Have I been touchy and sensitive toward those around me?

Have I hurt others by my flare-ups of anger and impatience?

Have I been quick to show my sorrow whenever I have
given pain to others, either consciously or inadvertently?

Have I contributed to the venial sins of others
by unreasonably teasing or annoying them?

Have I prevented others from performing
a good work by dissuading them from it?

Have I prayed for others, especially when
tempted to angry thoughts and feelings?

Have I prayed daily for my parents,
my family, and my benefactors?

The Hidden Power of Kindness

Do I treat my neighbors as I would have others
treat me by being kind and ready to help?

Do I think and act kindly toward all and
try to treat all alike, at least externally?

In dealing with my parents and superiors, am I respectful,
docile, and easy to get along with, like a good child?

Am I as polite and courteous to the members of
my family as I am to outsiders and guests?

Do I try to give a good example to all and, as far
as possible, to make them happy by sympathy, by kindly
conversation, and by a willingness to render little services?

∞

Prayer for Kindness

Keep us, O God, from pettiness;
let us be kind in thought, in word, and in deed.
Let us be done with faultfinding and leave off self-seeking.
May we put away all pretense and meet each other
face-to-face, without self-pity and without prejudice.
May we never be hasty in judgment and always generous.
Help us, O Lord, always to be kind.
Amen.

Lawrence G. Lovasik
(1913-1986)

"Life is short, and we must all give account of it on the Day of Judgment," said Fr. Lawrence Lovasik. "I am in earnest about using the time allotted to me by God on this earth to the best advantage in carrying out the ideal of my life — to make God more known and loved through my writings."[246]

The oldest of eight children, Lawrence Lovasik was born of Slovak parents in the steel-industry town of Tarentum, Pennsylvania. He was accepted into the Sacred Heart Mission Seminary in Girard, Pennsylvania, at the age of twelve and, after thirteen years of study and training, was ordained to the priesthood at St. Mary's Mission Seminary in Techny, Illinois, in 1938. Fr. Lovasik studied further at Rome's Gregorian Papal University, spent three years as a teacher and prefect of seminarians, and went on to do missionary work in America's coal and steel regions. In 1955, he founded the Sisters of the Divine Spirit, an American religious congregation of home and foreign missionaries whose services

---

[246] Walter Romig, *The Book of Catholic Authors*, 5th ser. (Grosse Pointe, Michigan: Walter Romig and Company, 1943), 181.

included teaching in schools and in catechetical classes, visiting homes, and assisting in social work.

Fr. Lovasik devoted much of his time to giving missions and retreats. These experiences and that of his earlier missionary work acquainted him with the spiritual needs, personal and family problems, and individual plans and longings of God's people, and he yearned to help them. Christ's exhortation to His first priests — "Go, and make disciples of all nations"[247] — was his inspiration. "I wanted to reach the hearts of people," he said, "but my voice could be heard only by those to whom I was able to preach."[248] Writing, he found, was his way to preach God's love and truth to the many, and it was his personal love for Christ, for the Blessed Mother, and for all immortal souls that drove him to dedicate as much time as possible to this talent.

Prayer and the Holy Eucharist are the emphases of many of the several books and more than fifty pamphlets that Fr. Lovasik wrote. His style is simple, sincere, and highly practical. He combines his vision of the transforming power of holiness and his compassionate understanding of man's desires and weaknesses to offer sound spiritual direction that motivates and inspires his readers, leads them step by step toward holiness, warns them against spiritual and temporal pitfalls, and guides them back to the right path when they go astray. Fr. Lovasik's wisdom not only reveals the often overlooked strength of holiness, but also continues to make real his life's ideal — to make God more known and loved.

[247] Matt. 28:19.
[248] Romig, *The Book of Catholic Authors*, 180.

∞

Sophia Institute Press®

Sophia Institute is a nonprofit institution that seeks to restore man's knowledge of eternal truth, including man's knowledge of his own nature, his relation to other persons, and his relation to God.

Sophia Institute Press® serves this end in numerous ways. It publishes translations of foreign works to make them accessible for the first time to English-speaking readers. It brings back into print books that have long been out of print. And it publishes important new books that fulfill the ideals of Sophia Institute.

These books afford readers a rich source of the enduring wisdom of mankind.

Sophia Institute Press® makes these high-quality books available to the general public by using advanced technology and by soliciting donations to subsidize its general publishing costs.

Your generosity can help Sophia Institute Press® to provide the public with editions of works containing the enduring wisdom of the ages. Please send your tax-deductible contribution to the address on the following page.